# Praise for
## *The Jesus Who Surprises*

"Dee is a voice in the wilderness, telling us of this Jesus who we long to ~~know~~ ~~but~~ often-times struggle to believe. We need her words, point~~ing~~

—SARA HAGERTY, author of E~~ ~~ ~~en:
*The Gift of Being Hidden in* ~~ ~~

"Sometimes the Bible can feel like a book of d~~ ~~ ~~ies, and we wonder how all the parts fit together. With wisdom and warmth, Dee Brestin guides us through the Old Testament, helping us understand how all the stories point to Jesus. *The Jesus Who Surprises* faithfully teaches the big picture of the Bible while offering daily encourage-ment to see God's work in our own stories."

—MELISSA KRUGER, director of women's content for the Gospel
Coalition and author of *In All Things: A Nine-Week Devotional
Bible Study on Unshakeable Joy*

"If you're looking for a unique Bible study that's immersed in powerful teaching, poignant stories, and thought-provoking discussion questions, *The Jesus Who Surprises* is for you. Dee Brestin skillfully weaves memorable truth throughout this well-written book while directing her readers to the discovery of Jesus in every part of life and in unexpected places throughout the Old and New Testaments. You can read this book on your own, or better yet, gather a group of your friends and experience this outstanding Bible study together. I highly recommend it!"

—CAROL KENT, speaker and author of *He Holds My Hand:
Experiencing God's Presence and Protection*

"This study has changed my life. I had so many misconceptions about who I thought God was before this, but I know now that He loves me beyond what I dreamed He could. My prayer life has completely changed, and I'm not afraid to be real with Him and know that He understands and cares about every little thing."

—JENNIFER GLAUBIUS

"If someone asked me if they should do this study, I would say, yes, 100 percent, go for it, because there are things in there I never saw before! This study will change your life and your perspective on the Bible.'"

—HOPE SIMS

## Praise for
## *He Calls You Beautiful*

"Dee Brestin has a lovely, lyrical writing voice, perfectly suited to the Song of Songs. Verse by verse, she engages each of our five senses to help us truly experience the breathtaking love of God. The resources and questions she offers for Bible studies are exceptional. And her sheer passion for Him captures our hearts and minds until we too are swept up in His divine dance. *He Calls You Beautiful* is just that—*beautiful.* I learned so much and loved every word!"

—Liz Curtis Higgs, best-selling author of *31 Verses to Write on Your Heart*

"Every woman's heart longs for her own personal love story in which she is desired, pursued, and cherished. As I read Dee's new book, *He Calls You Beautiful,* I wept again and again at the depth of love God has for me and for you. I underlined whole paragraphs so I could go back and read them again. If you long for your faith to move out of your head and into your heart, savor this book. You will feel undeniably loved."

—Leslie Vernick, Christian counselor, relationship coach, speaker, and author of numerous books including *The Emotionally Destructive Marriage*

"Dee Brestin joyfully leads readers through the enigmatic book of Song of Songs, causing our hearts to melt with the beauty of Christ and making us long for more intimacy with Christ."

—Nancy Guthrie, author of the Seeing Jesus in the Old Testament Bible study series

# THE
# JESUS
# WHO
# SURPRISES

## OTHER BOOKS BY DEE BRESTIN

*The Friendships of Women*
*He Calls You Beautiful*
*Idol Lies*
*The God of All Comfort*
*Falling in Love with Jesus (coauthored with Kathy Troccoli)*

## DEE'S BIBLE STUDIES SERIES

*A Woman of Wisdom*
*A Woman of Worship*
*A Woman of Contentment*
*A Woman of Love*
*A Woman of Beauty*

## FISHERMAN BIBLE STUDYGUIDES

*Examining the Claims of Jesus*
*Proverbs and Parables*
*Building Your House on the Lord*
*Friendship*

A full list of Dee's books and videos can be found
at www.deebrestin.com, or Google Dee Brestin Ministries.

# THE
# JESUS
# WHO
# SURPRISES

OPENING OUR EYES to HIS PRESENCE
in ALL of LIFE and SCRIPTURE

# DEE BRESTIN

Best-selling author of *The Friendships of Women*

MULTNOMAH

THE JESUS WHO SURPRISES

Details in some anecdotes and stories have been changed to protect the identities of the persons involved.

Trade Paperback ISBN 978-0-7352-9180-5
eBook ISBN 978-0-7352-9181-2

Cover design by Kelly L. Howard

Published in the United States by Multnomah, an imprint of the Crown Publishing Group, a division of Penguin Random House LLC, New York.

MULTNOMAH® and its mountain colophon are registered trademarks of Penguin Random House LLC.

Library of Congress Cataloging-in-Publication Data
Names: Brestin, Dee, 1944- author.
Title: The Jesus who surprises : opening our eyes to his presence in all of life and scripture / Dee Brestin.
Description: First edition. | Colorado Springs : Multnomah, [2019] | Includes bibliographical references.
Identifiers: LCCN 2018048488| ISBN 9780735291805 (pbk.) | ISBN 9780735291812 (ebook)
Subjects: LCSH: Jesus Christ—Textbooks. | Bible. Old Testament—Textbooks. |
    Spirituality—Christianity—Textbooks.
Classification: LCC BT207 .B74 2019 | DDC 232—dc23
LC record available at https://lccn.loc.gov/2018048488

Printed in the United States of America
2019—First Edition

10 9 8 7 6 5 4 3 2 1

SPECIAL SALES
Most Multnomah books are available at special quantity discounts when purchased in bulk by corporations, organizations, and special-interest groups. Custom imprinting or excerpting can also be done to fit special needs. For information, please email specialmarketscms@penguinrandomhouse.com or call 1-800-603-7051.

*Dedicated to Katherine Harrington, Miabelle Lano, Octavia Brestin, and Sadie Hale. These four daughters of my four daughters were born the same summer. How Jesus surprised us, turning our mourning into dancing!*

They said to each other, "Did not our hearts burn within us while he talked to us on the road, while he opened to us the Scriptures?"

—Luke 24:32

# Contents

## Part Three: How the Story Will End
### *The Prophets*

## Facilitator Resources

# How to Use This Book and Bible Study

Welcome! Whether you are reading this book on your own or in a small group, I pray that it will draw you closer to the God who surprises us with His love.

Each chapter in *The Jesus Who Surprises* is followed by an in-depth Bible study, so you have everything you need in one book. Plus, the study sections are divided into five days for the option to pace yourself throughout the week. What's more, you'll find free video lessons at deebrestin.com. Each video, running approximately fifteen minutes, corresponds to a chapter in the book and features teaching from Dee as well as testimonies from women impacted by the study. For those hungry to go deeper (the happiest people you'll meet!), there are other resources on the site, such as free sermons and music. You can also purchase DVDs from online websites. As valuable as I hope each chapter is, I believe that it is in God's Word where we find the greatest power for transformation and for joy!

If you are reading *The Jesus Who Surprises* in a small group and you just got your books at the first meeting, do the Get-Acquainted Bible Study on page 3. Then, for the next meeting, read chapter 1 and complete the first lesson ahead of time. But if your group already has the books and homework is complete, go right to discussing the first chapter and the first lesson.

For those leading a small group or Sunday school class through this study, read the facilitator notes in the back of this book in preparation for each gathering. You'll find suggestions for each lesson, deeper explanations of certain questions, and helpful hints for making your group the best it can be.

I look forward to journeying with you as we seek and find Jesus throughout Scripture and our lives!

# Optional Get-Acquainted Bible Study

1. Go around the group and share your name and an adjective that begins with the same letter your name does (for example, Introverted Ida, Teacher Tom, Dangerous Dee . . .). When it's your turn, say all the adjectives and names of the people who have gone before you as well!
2. Go around again and share something you are passionate about and why.
3. Jesus was always surprising people. Read these passages aloud, taking time to answer the questions as a group after each reading.

   Luke 4:16–22
   a. What observations or comments do you have? (Take time with this.)
   b. Why might Jesus's words and actions have surprised people?
   c. Consider what Isaiah says the Messiah would come to do. Have you experienced any of these benefits from Jesus? If so, explain.

   Luke 19:1–10
   a. What observations or comments do you have?
   b. Who is surprised by Jesus and why?
   c. What immediate changes do you see in Zacchaeus that suggest he is having a genuine conversion?
   d. Have you ever had a dramatic change in your life due to Jesus? If so, share.

Mark 4:35–41

    a. What observations or comments do you have?

    b. In verse 41, why do you think the disciples are "filled with great fear"?

    c. Have you ever had a moment when you felt great fear of God? If so, what was it like? Why did you feel fear?

4. The God Hunt![1] We'll go deeper into this in the book, but let's get our feet wet. Because Jesus is alive, He is still surprising us today, but we need to learn how to recognize His gifts and His mindfulness of us.

    a. Your most frequent way of spying God will come through realizing that "whatever is good and perfect is a gift . . . from God" (James 1:17, NLT). Let everything—from a perfect peach, to a kind clerk, to a lovely sunset—cause you to stop and thank Him. At the end of each day, record your best gift of the day. What might you say was your best gift yesterday?

    b. In Psalm 8:4, David looks at the heavens and then asks, "What is man that you are mindful of him?" Can you think of a time when you were quite sure God was being mindful of you—and were amazed?

    c. The richest groups are those where people are so hungry for God that they've done their homework. What is your plan for accomplishing your homework for this Bible study (when, where, how)?

# ONE

# A Journey of Surprises

## And Our Hearts Burned Within Us

> The passion children bring to hide-and-seek is the same
> passion we need to bring to finding God.
>
> —KAREN MAINS

When our sons reached grade-school age, they morphed the game hide-and-seek into "scare" hide-and-seek, surprising the seeker by leaping with a roar from the broom closet or the outdoor trash can. Or, if the stealthy seeker spied toes beneath the curtain or noticed a breathing blanket, he'd creep in and grab the hider with a bloodcurdling cry.

Our boys loved the adrenaline rush, but their little sister would often burst into tears. I'd say, "No more scare high-and-seek with Sally!"

Sally would protest, "Please, Mommy—I will be *brave* like my brothers this time. Let me play too!" If I relented and let her play, her terror and tears returned.

I wonder if Sally's feelings were akin to how we feel about Jesus sometimes. We *want* Him to show up, yet if He does, we're shocked and scared—similar to how the disciples felt when Jesus walked this earth. When a storm comes up with Jesus asleep in the stern, the disciples awaken Him and plead with Him to help. We are told that when He does, "they were filled with great fear" (Mark 4:41), suddenly more afraid of One who could stop a storm than of the storm itself.

That is how Dr. Jeff Johnson, my friend and neighbor, felt during one of his frequent medical mission trips to Honduras. On a Tuesday in July 1998, in Tegucigalpa, a young single mom brought her twelve-year-old daughter to the church, which had been transformed into a clinic for the week. She had taken Carla to six other clinics over the past several months. Each time Carla had been diagnosed with congenital glaucoma, the same medical condition that caused Ray Charles to go blind. It is permanent and irreversible. Jeff remembers the day well:

> Another doctor and I examined her and we formed the diagnosis. Her corneas were smoky white as a result of the extremely high eye pressure, and her eyes constantly wandered. She was unable to fixate on any object and unable to see the light from the flashlight.
>
> We spent time talking to the mother and told her there was no medical treatment available for her daughter. She had now heard the same diagnosis and prognosis for the seventh time.

The team hadn't prayed for her to be healed, yet as they were escorting her and her mother out, Jeff thought, *It wouldn't hurt.* The group surrounded the young girl, Jeff put his right hand over her eyes, and they began to pray.

He says, "I really don't remember specifically what we prayed, and I honestly did not expect anything to happen. After a few minutes, I removed my hand from her eyes and she exclaimed,

"'I can see!'

"My response was, 'What did you say?'

"'I can see!'

"We looked at each other, stunned in silent disbelief, while before our very eyes we witnessed a miracle. God had restored the visual pathways to her brain, and as the pressure normalized, her milky-white corneas became clear. As word of this spread through the packed clinic, a 'Holy Silence' swept through the building, for both Hondurans and North Americans alike."[1]

The German scholar Rudolf Otto used a Latin phrase for this "holy silence," this awe that people from all cultures feel when they come into the presence of One perfectly holy and powerful. He called it *mysterium tremendum et fascinans*. To quote Otto, this phrase means

- "Mysterium": wholly other, experienced with blank wonder, stupor
- "tremendum": awefulness, terror, absolute unapproachability . . .
- "fascinans": potent charm, attractiveness in spite of fear, terror, etc.[2]

We have an approach/avoidance reaction to God as we are drawn yet fearful as His holy presence makes us realize how sinful we are. As the old spiritual "Were You There?" says, "Sometimes it causes me to tremble, tremble, tremble."

Jeff had all those feelings the morning of the miracle: bountiful joy, a fearful awe, and a deep conviction of how often he may have short-circuited God's plan because of a preconceived notion of how He works.

I have come to believe that Jesus finds joy in surprising us but that often we are as blind spiritually as Carla was physically. We must ask Jesus to remove the veil from our eyes so we can see Him in every corner of Scripture and of life.

## Jesus in the Old Testament

My dear friend Ron came to Christ at the age of seventy, and he delights me with his continual surprise as he discovers things that for me have lost their luster through familiarity. I've told Ron I want to follow him around with a notepad because his reactions are so wonderful, so quotable! The other day in a Bible study he said, "I never knew before Jesus that you should listen to your wife." We burst into laughter. His wife, Debbie, grinned and said, "He's a changed man!"

Ron and Debbie recently took me to dinner at a restaurant on Lake Michigan. As we watched the waves roll in, Ron asked me what I was writing now.

"It's a book about how Jesus surprises us by turning up in the Old Testament and in our everyday lives."

Ron's fork stopped in midair. He raised his white furry eyebrows. "Jesus is in the Old Testament?"

I nodded. "Yes! Every prophet, priest, slain lamb, and suffering servant is a foreshadowing of Jesus, who is the ultimate prophet, priest, slain lamb, and suffering servant. But it is even more comprehensive than that. It isn't just that Jesus hides in every Old Testament book, but that *one* story—the story of His promised rescue—threads all the way through. God loved the Son so much, He created a bride for Him in Genesis 1. Then, when that bride was unfaithful, God had to rescue her. That story is the tapestry of the whole Bible, from Genesis through Revelation."

Ron shook his head: half amazement, half disbelief. I smiled, ready to mentally capture his response. "Dee, *how* do you know that?"

I told him about the Walk to Emmaus, my favorite New Testament story, where

Jesus Himself explains this truth. It occurs on the first Easter Sunday, at the end of Luke, when Jesus surprises two disciples on the road to Emmaus. It is here that Jesus reveals that we should be searching the whole Old Testament for Him and His redemptive gospel plan. And, just as it was for these two disciples (Luke 24:16, 31), a veil must be removed from our eyes or we will miss this surprising Jesus, both in the Old Testament and in our everyday lives.

## We Had Hoped He Was the One

Often we miss seeing Jesus in our lives because His behavior does not fit our expectations. The two on the road to Emmaus had expected deliverance from their political enemies, but now those very enemies had crucified Him. Who were these two disciples? At least one had to be named in order that this incident could be historically documented—and he is: Cleopas, though he is not named anywhere else in Scripture. And suggestions abound on the identity of the other disciple. Some think it is the wife of Cleopas, but we simply do not know. There is more detail in this resurrection account than in most, lending credence to the belief that Luke's source was these two disciples themselves. (Luke 1:2 tells us Luke received his accounts from eyewitnesses, and it is fascinating to me that there are more women's stories in Luke than in any other gospel, so some of those eyewitnesses must have been women.)

A "stranger" who comes up beside them asks, "What is this conversation that you are holding with each other as you walk?" (24:17).

They stand still. "Are you the only visitor to Jerusalem who does not know the things that have happened there in these days?" (verse 18).

Jesus asks them simply, "What things?"

They reply, "Concerning Jesus of Nazareth . . . and how our chief priests and rulers delivered him up to be condemned to death, and crucified him. But we had hoped that he was the one to redeem Israel" (verses 19–21).

Then the two tell Him that "it is now the third day" (verse 21) since all this happened. In Jewish thought, the third day was the day of deliverance. On the third day, Abraham saw the ram in the thicket and Jonah was delivered from the fish. Jesus Himself had told His disciples He was going to Jerusalem to suffer, be killed, and on the third day be raised (Matthew 16:21).

Yet it's the third day, and they think there's been no deliverance. Jesus listens to them describe the "idle tale" of their women (Luke 24:11), who claimed that Christ had risen from the dead. (The Greek word Luke the physician uses that is translated "idle tale" is a medical term meaning "the delirious talk of the very ill"!)

At this, Jesus exclaims, "O foolish ones, and slow of heart to believe all that the prophets have spoken! Was it not necessary that the Christ should suffer these things and enter into his glory?" (verses 25–26).

Then, "beginning with Moses and all the Prophets, he interpreted to them in *all* the Scriptures the things concerning himself" (verse 27, emphasis added).

The figure of speech "from Moses . . . to all the prophets" is called *zeugma* and means *all* their Scriptures from "front to back."[3] In other words, Jesus shows them how *every* book of the Bible they have at the time is about the Christ and what He came to do.

Yet it isn't until they are breaking bread together that evening that Jesus lifts the spiritual veil from their eyes and allows them to recognize Him (verses 30–31). Oh, what a reunion! He whom they thought was dead is alive, and they can see, hear, and touch Him again!

Later they marvel, "Did not our hearts burn within us while he talked to us on the road, while he opened to us the Scriptures?" (verse 32).

## Did Not Our Hearts Burn Within Us?

Just as the disciples did, when we discover Jesus in unexpected places, "our hearts burn within us" and indeed we are transformed. John Piper says, "Beholding *is* becoming," [4] referencing 2 Corinthians 3:18: "And we all, with unveiled face, beholding the glory of the Lord, are being transformed into the same image from one degree of glory to another."

The Spirit does a supernatural work in us when we behold the glory of the Lord. When I spy Jesus or His gospel in the Old Testament, my heart melts. Why? Awe comes over me as I see how *every* book in the Bible is about Jesus and His rescue. Over more than a thousand years, many holy men, from many cultures and places, though usually working independently of one another, told the *same* story. How could this be? It is because almighty God Himself is behind the various personalities telling this One Story, this story of His quest to rescue the family He loves.

Sally Lloyd-Jones, in *The Jesus Storybook Bible,* puts it like this:

It's an adventure story about a young Hero who comes from a far country to win back his lost treasure. It's a love story about a brave Prince who leaves his palace, his throne—everything—to rescue the one he loves. It's like the most wonderful of fairy tales that has come true in real life![5]

This same Jesus who rescued His people back then is still rescuing us today. Often He appears when we are at our lowest, facing shattered dreams. He *may* surprise us, just as He did for the two on the road to Emmaus, by turning our sorrow into joy. Or He may show up when we least expect Him in answers to prayer, in timing that is too unusual to be coincidence, or through the sense of His holy presence.

I pray that through this book, God will lift a veil from your eyes so that you might more frequently encounter Jesus in Scripture and in life. At the close of each chapter is an in-depth Bible study to help you discover Jesus and His gospel for yourself. Whether on your own or in a small group, you will learn how to go on a daily God Hunt to see Him where you might have missed Him before, just as the two disciples on the road to Emmaus saw Him where they least expected Him.

Luke 24:44, Jesus mentions three representative divisions of the three main sections of the Old Testament: Moses, the Psalms, and the Prophets. Therefore, I am dividing this book and study into those three parts:

1. Books of Moses: representing the historical books of Genesis through Esther
2. Psalms: representing the poetical books of Job through the Song of Songs
3. Prophets: representing the prophetical books of Isaiah through Malachi

When we study the historical books (staying primarily in Genesis), we will see how the story begins: the beautiful music of creation, the song as it becomes discordant, and then the melody of hope reminding us that all is not lost.

When we study the poetical books (staying primarily in the Psalms), we learn how to live in this story, this fallen world, so that despite the sorrow, we may know an inextinguishable joy.

When we study the prophetic books (staying primarily in Isaiah), we will see how the story is going to end. When we realize how accurate Isaiah's prophecies were concerning the first coming of the Messiah, our confidence will grow in the accuracy of his prophecies for the second coming of our Messiah and his prophecies of heaven.

## Why the Big Picture Matters

Recently I counseled a young woman who was distressed because her parents, who once seemed so grounded in Scripture, had been swept up into false teaching. She said, "They are so sure that this new teaching is the truth and that they were wrong before. How can we know for sure what's true and what is not?"

This is such an important question, and one of the main reasons I wanted to write this book.

I told her, "We need to take Paul's warning to Timothy to heart, about 'rightly handling the word of truth' [2 Timothy 2:15]. The word *handling* in the Greek is *orthotomeo,* an engineering term that refers to keeping things straight, aligned—small pieces must fit into the unified whole. God doesn't disagree with Himself. Any doctrine you embrace must fit into the unified themes of the Bible. The reason, for example, that we don't believe that something must be added to our faith to save us, as your parents now do, is that the whole theme of the Bible is that the blood of Jesus is sufficient to make the vilest sinner clean. The reason we don't believe that Jesus is just a great teacher or prophet—as Jehovah's Witnesses, Mormons, and Christian Scientists do—is that the whole theme of the Bible is that He is very God of very God."

I went on to explain that when a verse doesn't seem to fit into the unified whole, it is only an *apparent* contradiction. Either God will make it clear when we see Him face to face, or light will be given to you as you hold it up to the unified themes of the Bible.

For example, in Galatians 5:19–21, Paul gives a list of sins and closes with "Those who do such things will not inherit the kingdom of God." This, out of context, could lead some to think that if they *don't* do such things, they will automatically go to heaven. But this interpretation cannot be correct because the unified theme of the whole Bible and of Galatians itself says we are saved only by faith in Christ, not by our actions or inactions.

Failing to see that the Bible is one great story is like failing to look at the cover of a puzzle box before you dive into its one thousand pieces. You may be able to put together the puzzle, but it will be frustrating. You will often be trying to push a piece of the blue lake into the blue sky. How much wiser to first look at the cover! And what treasures we discover when we journey through the Old Testament with Jesus in mind.

In this journey you will see the same themes appearing and reappearing, equipping you to spot teachings that run like beautiful threads throughout Scripture. And I know, like the two on the road to Emmaus, your heart will burn within you as you begin to spy Jesus in the Old Testament and in every corner of your life.

# Bible Study One

As a group, view the related video and share comments: go to deebrestin.com and click on *The Jesus Who Surprises* under Free Teaching Videos. Also, as an option for going deeper, listen online (Google it) to "Jesus Vindicated" by Tim Keller.

## Icebreakers
*Skip questions 1 and 3 if you did the Optional Get-Acquainted Bible Study.*
1.  Go around the group and share your name and an adjective that begins with the same letter your name does (for example, Introverted Ida, Teacher Tom, Dangerous Dee . . .). When it's your turn, say all the adjectives and names of the people who have gone before you as well!
2.  Why have you come to this study group, and what do you hope to see happen here?
3.  What could you do to help make this discussion group the best it could be?

## Week One God Hunt
Each day record your best gift of the day in a sentence: *Today I spied God when* . . . (It could be an encouraging email, a good day at work, the kids going back to school!) At the end of the week, put a star next to your *best* gift of the week to share with others in your group.

## Day One: Chapter Review
4.  Read the chapter and highlight as you read. Write down one thought that impressed you so you can share it with the group. (Always go around the group with this question, giving freedom to pass.)

5. For those who listened to the Tim Keller sermon, what stood out to you the most about his words?

*Today I spied God when . . .*

## Day Two: The Context of the Walk to Emmaus

Read Luke 24:1–12. (Do this as homework, but when you meet in the group have some-one read it aloud and then pause before the questions and ask for comments. God often shows up during these times of looking at the Word together.)

If you were making up this story in the days of Jesus, you wouldn't have women as witnesses. Women were not considered credible witnesses at that time. Yet God values women and had them first at the empty tomb. Luke, who wants to give an orderly ac-count (1:1–4), reports this incident exactly as it happened.

6. What comments or observations do you have after reading or listening to this passage?

7. The word translated "nonsense" or "idle tale" in 24:11 is actually a medical term that Luke the physician uses, meaning "the delirious talk of the very ill." Why do you think this is the disciples' initial reaction even though the women report exactly what Jesus has said would happen?

8. Did any verse become "radioactive"? In other words, did a verse or phrase send off a powerful charge to you spiritually and cause you to pause? (We'll be considering this question often in our studies, as God so often speaks to us

through our initial, unguarded reaction to something in His Word.) If so, meditate on those words to see what God might be saying to you. What stands out to you as you meditate on them?

*Today I spied God when . . .*

## Day Three: First Look at the Walk to Emmaus

9. As an overview, read Luke 24:13–35 carefully twice and write down any observations, comments, or questions. Did anything become radioactive? Read it aloud again in the group and take turns sharing comments.

*Today I spied God when . . .*

## Day Four: Going Deeper with the Walk to Emmaus

In this retelling of the two disciples meeting Christ while walking to Emmaus, we find humor, pathos, and a deep sense of reality—this truly happened.

10. Read Luke 24:15–24.

a. What emotions might the two on the way to Emmaus have had as they were walking? What might they have been talking about?

b. What emotions might Jesus have had as He walked alongside these two? Why?

c. Why do you think Jesus asks them what happened (verse 19)?

11. Read Luke 24:25–27.

a. What does Jesus say they should have known, and why? Do you believe Jesus is angry with the two for needing Him to teach them? Why or why not?

b. What does He reveal to them about their Scriptures (the Old Testament)?

12. Read Luke 24:28–35.

*a. What might have felt familiar to the two about this scene?

b. How do the two express their emotions after Jesus vanishes from their sight?

c. It is still night, but what do they do and why?

d. What words would you use to describe the scene of the two telling the others that they have seen the risen Lord? What sounds, emotions, exclamations, and questions might have been a part of that moment?

e. What does the resurrection of Christ mean to you personally?

f. Did any verse in this story become radioactive to you? If so, explain.

*13. Briefly share a moment in your life when Jesus became particularly real to you, when your heart burned within you, whether at the time of your salvation or another time.

*Today I spied God when . . .*

## Day Five: The Gospel in the Old Testament

Read Luke 24:36–46. With His new, resurrected body, Jesus could simply disappear and appear, and while the eleven were talking, He appears before them, allows them to touch Him, and eats fish to show He is not a ghost. Then He again turns to the Old Testament—their Scriptures—and shows them how He and His gospel are in it.

14. Describe what happened in this scene.

*15. What three sections of the Old Testament does Jesus open to and explain, according to Luke 24:44? Since the Greek word *zeugma,* translated "all," means everything from front to back, explain how the three categories represent the whole Old Testament.

16. Not only will you see Jesus foreshadowed in people like Adam, Job, Ruth, David, Esther, and others, but you will also discover the foreshadowing of God's planned rescue, or the gospel, throughout the Old Testament. How does Jesus explain this in both Luke 24:26 and Luke 24:46?

*17. The term *mysterium tremendum* describes how we feel in the presence of the holy. The two on the road to Emmaus felt it. Have you ever sensed it? If so, when?

*Today I spied God when . . .*

## Prayer Time

Take time to give thanks. You can do this with your eyes open! The facilitator will go around the circle and invite you to share your best God Hunt from the week or one takeaway from the lesson or discussion as a way of thanking God for being personal with you. You also have the freedom to pass. You may want to plan ahead what you will share. If so, write it here:

# PART ONE

# How the Story Began

## *The Books of Moses*

# Two

# The God of the Dance

## *Surprised by Love*

> It dawned on me for the first time, really. It had dawned on
> me before, but it really sank in: the Christmas story. . . .
> Tears came down my face, and I saw the genius of this. . . .
> There must be an incarnation. Love must be made flesh.
>
> —BONO

When our son JR was little, he liked to give me choices such as "Would you rather be run over by a tractor or a steamroller?"

"Neither," I'd say.

"Mommy, you have to choose."

Many adults who come to Christ feel caught between what seems like two hard choices. They come to faith fearfully, not knowing what God will demand of them but deciding that whatever it is, is better than hell. C. S. Lewis seemed to identify with "a prodigal who is brought in kicking, struggling, resentful, and darting his eyes in every direction for a chance of escape."[1] But still, he came—fearful of *not* surrendering to the truth.

But then! C. S. Lewis was "surprised by joy"! Likewise, John Wesley said, "I felt my heart strangely warmed;"[2] Chuck Colson was so overcome by his tears that he couldn't back his car out of his friend's driveway;[3] and Anne Lamott says, "Something inside me that was stiff and rotting" became "soft and tender."[4]

But perhaps my favorite story of receiving Christ comes from Karla Faye Tucker, a convicted murderer in a Texas prison who considered Christianity a "weak thing." Yet when a Christian ministry came into the prison, curiosity caused Karla to "steal" a Bible from their table, not realizing the Bibles were free. Then she hid in the corner of her cell so that no one would see her reading a Bible. She describes what she did next:

> I opened the Bible and started reading. I don't know how long it took, but I remember that I was kneeling on the floor, crying, asking God to come into my heart and to forgive me for what I had done. . . . I knew no matter what I had done, I was loved, just like that, just like I was. That's when the whole weight of what I had done fell on me. I realized for the first time that I had brutally murdered two people and there were people hurting out there because of me. Yet God was saying, "I love you." . . . At that moment, He reached down inside of me and ripped out that violence at the very roots and poured Himself in.[5]

All of these individuals were surprised not only by God's love for them but also by a new love welling up in their hearts for others. Karla had the vision for Discipleship Unlimited, a prison ministry that has reduced the recidivism (rate of return) to 2 percent in eleven Texas prisons for inmates who have gone through its program. Even as she waited for her execution, Karla was writing down last-minute ideas for the ministry.[6]

Why is it that adults who come to Christ often have this sense of love, joy, and power enveloping them, whereas converts to other religions seldom do?

## The Perichoresis

It is in the beginning, in the account of creation, where we first spy the hidden Jesus. And it is there, when we see the dance of the Trinity, that we begin to see why our God alone is love.

The Father, the Son, and the Holy Spirit have been in loving fellowship from before the beginning. The early church fathers had a name for this "dance." They called it the *perichoresis*. Do you see the music in the word?

By contrast, the gods of other religions are either warring gods or single-person gods. In Islam, for example, we see some tension here. One of the ninety-nine names given to Allah is "the Loving." Theologian Michael Reeves observes, "But how could Allah be loving in eternity? Before he created there was nothing else in existence that he could love (and the title does not refer to self-centered love but love for others)."[7] Single-person gods could not have been love from all eternity, for they had no one to love. Nor could they be fathers, for they had no children. Monolithic gods are more like cosmic police officers: solitary, curved in on themselves, watching for transgressions. Their followers have joined a march rather than a dance.

You can see the dance among three persons of the Trinity in the opening words of Genesis: there's God, there's God the Spirit hovering over the face of the earth, and there's God the Word speaking the world into creation. (When we get to John's gospel, we learn the Word is Jesus Christ.) So we have one God in three persons, and then God says, "Let us make man in our image" (Genesis 1:26).

Do you see Jesus hidden in the pronouns? We are made in the image of the Trinity, and because our God is relational, we are relational as well.

Puritan Richard Sibbes wrote that the Father, the Son, and the Holy Ghost were happy in themselves and enjoyed one another before they created the world but that this kind of love cannot help but spread. He spoke of the living God as a life-giving, warming sun who delights "to spread his beams and his influence in inferior things, to make all things fruitful. Such a goodness is in God as is in a fountain, or in the breast that loves to ease itself of milk."[8]

Because our triune God wanted to spread His love, He made man in His image. And because we are the image of God, we, like Him, long to be in relationship. As Augustine said in *The Confessions,* "Thou hast formed us for Thyself, and our hearts are restless till they find rest in Thee."

Attempts to explain the personal Trinity with impersonal objects like an egg or an apple fall short. But comparing the Trinity to a dance, with three loving beings in harmony, or to a marriage (the metaphor Scripture gives) comes closer. In marriage you have two similar yet different persons becoming one, joining in a dance of love. And just as husband and wife generally share a love that overflows and desires children, so does our triune God.

## "The Risenness of Jesus"

As a young mother, when I rose from my knees after putting my trust in Christ, I too was overwhelmed at the love He poured into my heart and the difference in the way I saw *everything.* Jesus describes this in John 3:7 as being "born again," and Ezekiel speaks of God putting a new spirit within us, changing our hearts of stone into hearts of flesh (Ezekiel 36:26–27).

Brennan Manning called this power "the risenness of Jesus,"[9] for the same power that raised Jesus from the dead has come to live in us, if we have become His children. Yet so often, instead of depending on His wisdom and power, we return to our old ways of depending on our own wisdom and power.

To illustrate, consider two ways of praying. One is to come up with a grocery list of things *we* want, praying in our own wisdom. Another is to seek, through Scripture, what *He* wants for us and then ask Him for it! George Müller found his prayer time was transformed when, instead of praying and then reading the Bible, he reversed the order and allowed the Scripture he studied for that day to guide his prayers.[10]

Since we are in the beginning of Genesis, let's consider something we learn about God's will for our lives and then see how to take the hand of the Lord of the dance to experience His power.

## It Is Not Good for Man to Be Alone

Made in the image of a triune relational God, we need fellowship not only with our Maker but also with one another. Most of us desire marriage, and all of us need friendship, whether we realize it or not. We may realize we get grumpy when we are deprived of sleep or food, but we may not realize that we get grumpy when we are deprived of fellowship.

When God considers Adam, alone in Eden, with only animals for company, He declares, "It is not good that the man should be alone" (Genesis 2:18). Adam doesn't know what he's missing, but the One who made him does. It isn't until God brings Eve to Adam that he realizes his need and breaks out into song:

> This at last is bone of my bones
> and flesh of my flesh.
> —verse 23

It is not good for either gender to be alone, nor is it wise to expect your spouse to meet all of your needs. Women are more apt to understand their need for friends than are men, but the most spiritually mature men I know have come to trust God's exhortations for fellowship and seek it out with other godly men.

When I find a kindred-spirit friend, though I don't actually break out into song as Adam did, my heart *is* singing. One of my favorite books is Wallace Stegner's *Crossing to Safety,* based on the actual friendship he and his wife found with another couple. He describes the night that it all began, when he came home to find his wife and this "Harvard/Smith woman obviously enjoying cinnamon toast and Lipton's Orange Pekoe in our basement."[11] He watched, feeling a bit like an intruder, as they continued their animated conversation. Then the new friend revealed she was pregnant.

> "Pregnant?" Sally said. "You too? When? When is it due?"
> 
> "Not till March. And are *you*? When's yours?"
> 
> "The same time!" . . .
> 
> She and Sally fell on each other. You never saw two more delighted people.
> 
> If they had been twins separated in infancy, and now revealed to one another by
> 
> some birthmark or other perepetia, they couldn't have been more exhilarated.[12]

How I remember meeting Ann Dahl within months of moving to Fargo, North Dakota. I had prayed for God to help me not to be alone—that is, without a woman friend, in Fargo. And then I stayed alert for His answer.

Soon after our move, I interviewed Ann for a writing project and indeed we both sensed a strong connection. Ann told me how T. S. Eliot's poem "The Hollow Men" impacted her in college.

"I didn't want to be hollow, and I needed to find out if Jesus was the answer to the meaninglessness of my life." I grinned at her like the Cheshire Cat in *Alice's Adventures in Wonderland,* thinking, *You too? You love Eliot? You wanted to escape meaninglessness too?* I was already thanking God for the gift I was quite sure He was giving me. And then, in taking God's hand in the dance, I risked reaching out to Ann again, letting her know I was pursuing her in friendship, and God not only knit our souls together but also brought Sylvia, Ann's closest friend, into our threefold cord. Thirty-five years later, Ann, Sylvia, and I are still finishing one another's sentences and strengthening one another in God. To paraphrase Stegner, it is as if we recognized some kind of birthmark in one another.

When I study friendship in Scripture, I realize how those who were alert to the leading of God and risked following Him in the dance were the ones who found kindred-spirit friends.

Ruth followed God's lead to go all the way to Bethlehem with Naomi, Jonathan recognized a kindred-spirit friend in David and pledged himself to him, and Mary, after listening carefully to Gabriel, *hurried* across seventy miles to spend three months with Elizabeth. And what God did thousands of years ago, He is still doing.

Pam, a petite, pretty young mother, showed up at my study as I was testing *The Jesus Who Surprises*. It was her first Bible study, and she opened up to Scripture like a budding rose opens to the warmth of the sun. One day she told us her story.

Eleven months after her first son was born, her second son was born. Overwhelmed by the constant demands of two babies, Pam was often in tears. This dramatic change in lifestyle has brought many a young mother down, and while this analogy has its flaws, it may be akin to Adam's feelings when his days were filled with beautiful animals over whom God had given him dominion and care but with whom he could not carry on a conversation.

Pam fought her depression, going faithfully to the gym in the hopes that exercise would release endorphins and help her feel better. One day on the treadmill, emotions welled up again, and she fled to the locker room, hiding in a corner, wiping her eyes with Kleenex, hoping no one would see her. When she couldn't stop crying, she decided to get dressed and go home.

When Pam came out of the dressing room, she found this note pinned to her backpack: "I'm not sure what you are going through right now, but just know you are a child of God and deserve to find your place in this world."

As a devout Catholic, Pam believed in God. The note seemed to speak directly to her and her specific struggle, for she had not felt fulfilled as a stay-at-home mom. That note led her to call out to God for help.

And help began to come, because indeed Jesus hears our cries and knows what we need. First, Pam felt led to go to a therapist, who stressed the importance of self-care. "That," Pam said, "got me in a position to say yes to what God brought next."

One December night, Pam's husband, Chris, gave her a break and took the boys out for pizza. Then they went to an adjoining park, where colorful Christmas lights had been erected over wire hoops to form a long beautiful tunnel. The boys were racing and laughing through the lights and connected, as children will, with another little boy. The parents of that little boy, Dave and Gretta, began to converse easily with Chris, beginning with the realization that they each had named a son Elijah.

A spark of friendship was lit. The adults exchanged phone numbers, and soon the four parents got together. They *did* enjoy one another immensely, so Gretta took a risk and invited Pam to my Bible study, explaining to her that I was testing a study I was writing. Having never been in a Bible study before, Pam was hesitant, and Gretta didn't push, trusting God would bring her if this was His plan.

Pam wondered, *I've never studied the Bible before. Will I look stupid? Should I do this? Will my boys be okay in their childcare?* Her husband, who was also Catholic, had known a rich experience of fellowship with other believers who were not Catholic through a campus ministry, so he encouraged Pam to go, believing it would be so good for her to take time for herself and to be encouraged by God and sisters in Christ.

That resonated with what her therapist had told her, so Pam decided to take the risk and step out on faith. She told me later that the very first day she came, she knew this was what had been missing in her spiritual life and road to recovery. She felt a connection with the women, was inspired by their relationships with Jesus, and longed to improve her own relationship with Him.

Even though I have seen God transform hearts so many times, it always leaves me in wonder—it's like the first snowfall each winter, or the first crocus pushing through the frozen ground each spring. I sensed Pam's tender heart right away and felt led to affirm that in front of the whole group. She kept coming, kept flowering, and we all witnessed God helping His child find her "place in this world."

When you have cried out to God for a kindred-spirit friend and you have an encounter in which He seems to be answering that prayer, you feel as giddy as a child on Christmas morning. You are reflecting the image of God that we see in the Trinity in Genesis 1—and taking God's hand and joining with Him in the dance!

But I must tell you it doesn't always happen that way, for reasons only God knows. God doesn't always leap out, giving us exactly what we want. He's not a vending machine—we can't put in a request and expect the answer to just drop down.

Sometimes it is just as surprising how long God makes us wait, seeming to hide His face when we feel we need Him the most.

## When God's Love Hides

After my husband, Steve, died of cancer, I eventually moved to the cabin I inherited from my parents in Door County, Wisconsin. The moving van arrived on November 1. The beautiful autumn leaves were gone and so were all the tourists. There were no families on the beach, hikers on the trails, or even cars on the road as I drove to get groceries at Piggly Wiggly. I thought, *What have I done?* I went to the church that I had attended in summers past, a church that was always bursting at the seams with people. Now, without tourists, it was nearly empty, with just a handful of people scattered in two pews. I panicked. *I am going to be a widow in the woods in the winter in Wisconsin, starving for fellowship.*

My sister, who spent summers in Door County, told me of a conversation she'd had with a local artist who told her he'd enjoyed the biography Eric Metaxas wrote of Dietrich Bonhoeffer. I thought, *Perhaps that means he and his wife are Christians.*

One day when I was about to bike to the cemetery, I knew I would pass their house. So I prayed, *Lord, despite the cold day, if either the husband or wife happens to be outside, I'll take it as a sign and stop and talk to them.* And sure enough, as I approached, I saw the wife filling their bird feeder. I hopped off my bike, put the kickstand down, and began to walk briskly toward her, hopeful and excited. But when she looked up, she didn't smile. Instead, I felt like she had a flashing No Trespassing sign on her forehead. My excitement drained. But I was halfway across her lawn and there was no turning back. I tried to find courage, telling myself, *As soon as she knows I'm not a cult member or collecting for charity, she'll warm up.*

As I got close I gave her my biggest smile and said, "Hi, I'm your neighbor but we've never met, so I wanted to introduce myself. My name is Dee Brestin."

Silence.

*Awkward.* I talked faster. "You know my sister Bonnie Rock. She told me your husband had liked the biography on Bonhoeffer, and I thought we might share the same faith."

"We do not." Stony glare.

I froze. What to say next? How could I possibly turn this conversation around into something more pleasant?

"Oh, my mistake. Well . . . I like to feed the birds too." *Lame.* Now I was stammering. "I, I, just moved here and it's nice to meet you." I put out my hand, but she didn't take it.

I took my hand back. *Help me, God.* "I'm sorry to have bothered you." I stood there like a fool, trying to think of a nice exit, but I was as frozen and silent as those turned to stone by the White Witch of Narnia.

She stared at me, willing me to leave.

So I turned and bolted to my bike. I pedaled away furiously. Once I knew she couldn't see me, I dropped my bike, collapsed into the bushes, and wept. *Lord, what was that about? Have I lost my mind? So starved for friends that I've turned into a stalker?*

I still don't know why this woman responded to me as she did—perhaps I was too aggressive, especially with someone married to a well-known artist. I may never know why she was so cold, but I do know that God permitted it. He is a God who often makes us wait despite our desperate pleadings for what we think are very reasonable requests. Why?

A light came on for me a few years later as I was studying how Jesus is hidden in the Song of Songs. This earthly love story points to the ultimate love story, that of Christ and His bride. A metaphor that the bride uses in this Song to describe her beloved has penetrated my heart and helped me to trust Him when He hides.

Separated from her love, the bride is gladdened to hear his voice:

The voice of my beloved!
    Behold, he comes,
leaping over the mountains,
    bounding over the hills.
My beloved is like a gazelle
    or a young stag.
—2:8–9

St. John of the Cross, who lived in Spain in the fifth century, commented on the swiftness with which the deer shows and hides himself in this passage and how that is an apt analogy to our Lord:

It is noteworthy that in the Song of Songs the bride compares the Bridegroom to the stag. . . . She makes this comparison . . . because of the swiftness with which he shows and then hides himself. He usually visits devout souls in order to gladden and liven them, and then leaves in order to try, humble, and teach them.[13]

But whether He leaps out or hides, it is love that motivates Him. Joni Eareckson Tada, who prayed for many years for healing from quadriplegia, and also from breast cancer, has trusted His mysterious ways and has ministered to so many of us through her writing, speaking, and art. She writes, "God cares most—not about making us comfortable—but about teaching us to hate our sins, grow up spiritually, and love him."[14]

He is a surprising God, both in the times He delights us and in the times He hides. But whatever He chooses, it is for our best, for He promises to make all things beautiful in His time (Ecclesiastes 3:11).

As we see from the beginning of Scripture, He is the God of the dance, the God who gave up His only Son for us, and the God whose power brought that Son back from the dead. All these truths will sustain us as we consider another surprising aspect of our God: His severity. For, indeed, those who think of Jesus as meek and mild have not read the gospel accounts of Him—or the powerful references to His passion that we find even back in Genesis. That's what we're going to look at next.

## Bible Study Two

As a group, view the related video and share comments: go to deebrestin.com and click on *The Jesus Who Surprises* under Free Teaching Videos. Also, as an option for going deeper, listen online to "Why the Trinity Is So Delightful" by Michael Reeves.

### Week Two God Hunt

Continue to record your daily God Hunts of thanksgiving. This week be particularly alert to the power of Christ in your life. In Philippians 3:10, Paul speaks of his longing to "know him and the power of his resurrection." Brennan Manning calls this "the risenness of Christ" in your life. For example, you might notice evidence of transformation in an area of your life, an answer to prayer in a relationship, or wisdom in a challenging situation at work. Then, at the end of the week, highlight your best God Hunt to share with the group.

## Day One: Chapter Review

1. Read the chapter and highlight as you read. Write down two thoughts that impressed you.

2. If you listened to the sermon by Michael Reeves, share what stood out to you.

3. Many adults who come to Christ have an approach/avoidance reaction: Nicodemus came under cover of night, while C. S. Lewis came kicking and screaming. Why do you think that is? Can you identify with that reaction?

*Today I spied God when . . .*

## Day Two: Before the Beginning There Was Love

4. Read John 1:1–5. What do you learn about Jesus from this passage? How might this differ from what most people assume about Jesus or from the assumptions we make about Him?

5. Do you remember when you first realized Jesus was God? If so, share briefly.

6. Read Genesis 1:1–2. How can you see the Father and the Spirit here?

7. Read Genesis 1:26. How can you see the Father and the Son here?

8. Try explaining the Trinity in a few sentences using the metaphor of either a dance or a marriage.

*Today I spied God when . . .*

## Day Three: Love by Its Very Nature Spreads

9. Think about the last time you discovered a great book, restaurant, or movie. Did you want to share this "love"? If so, what did you do?

10. Read 1 John 1:1–4. Describe John's excitement and desire to share it with others.

11. Who were some of the first people to share Jesus with you? Why do you think they did?

12. Has there been a time when you met someone and sensed an instantaneous bond because of what you share in Christ? If so, share something about that time.

13. Historical accounts tell us John was severely persecuted and the other eleven apostles martyred for sharing their faith. Why do you think they told others about Jesus despite the risk?

*Today I spied God when . . .*

## Day Four: It Is Not Good for Man to Be Alone

*14. Read Genesis 1:27 and then reflect on some of the ramifications of being made in the image of a triune God. Why do only male and female together complete the image of God? What longings do you have for relationship?

15. Read Genesis 2:18–25. What stands out to you the most about this passage?

16. When you have moved to a new area, how did you find friends in Christ? Do you have a story of God meeting you during this time?

17. How has God blessed you recently through Christian fellowship? Explain.

*Today I spied God when . . .*

## Day Five: When God's Love Hides

It is exciting when we spy God at work, but other times He seems distant, or even hidden. On the road to Emmaus, Jesus hides His identity from the two for a time. In the book of Job, though God did appear to Job three times, most of the time He is silent.

*18. What might be some reasons that God would be silent or hide from His child?

*19. When have you experienced the silence or hiddenness of God? How did you respond, and how do you view this time now, in retrospect?

*Today I spied God when . . .*

## *Prayer Time*

Made in the image of a triune God, we crave meaningful fellowship. That can happen both in study together and in prayer together, especially when people are willing to be vulnerable in sharing their own needs and in listening carefully to others. Each week your facilitator will lead you in an exercise to help you have a meaningful prayer time together.

If your group is larger than six, cluster in smaller circles. With eyes open, share one God sighting from last week as a way of praising God. After everyone has shared, vocalize one way you *personally* need God's help this coming week. Then bow your heads and one facilitator will lift up names for short sentence prayers.

# THREE

# He Showed Up with a Whip

## Surprised by Severity

> The first fruit of sin is you are cut off from God and feel
> trauma in His presence. . . . If you've never felt that, then
> your comfy God is not the real God, but a god you have
> created in your mind.
>
> —TIM KELLER

The same God who surprises us with His love surprises us with His severity. How I remember when He showed up at a Christian booksellers convention a number of years ago. I felt like Jesus had arrived with His whip to bring us all to our senses.

I was a young writer, and it was my first convention. Since it was in Orlando, we made it a family trip, planning to take in Disney World as well. At the convention, we were all a little starstruck, for celebrities were everywhere, autographing books, CDs, and footballs. When we stood in line for Kenneth Taylor to autograph *The Living Bible*, my daughter Sally said, "I thought God wrote the Bible!"

It would take days to peruse the booths that seemed to run endlessly in the mammoth arena. There were exciting new books, creative curriculums, and rows and rows dedicated to just music.

But then there was the more carnival-like side: booths selling bumper stickers, T-shirts, "holy" anointing oil from Israel, wallpaper, and yo-yos imprinted with the words of John 3:16. When I stopped at a booth featuring Christian comics, I remembered a biting essay my nephew Peter Rock had written for the magazine *Tin House*.

Peter is witty, charming, and a gifted author. (His book *My Abandonment* has been made into a stunning movie called *Leave No Trace,* which premiered at both Sundance and Cannes.) Though I have tried to give scholarly books on Christianity to Peter, such as Tim Keller's *The Reason for God,* he refused them, explaining he was not interested. He gibes that my sister Sally has been using her age as an excuse to forget her promise *not* to send him Christian books. I wonder if Peter has been turned off, in part, by the crass materialism of some who proclaim the name of Christ.

The assignment from *Tin House* was to write an essay "on the piece of literature that first awakened his libido." While I probably would have written about *Gone with the Wind* from when I was in seventh grade, Peter wrote about reading *Archie* comics when he was seven. Peter and his sister had discovered a cache of comic books at his aunt's cabin on Kangaroo Lake in Wisconsin. In his article, Peter refers to the "Christian" edition of *Archie* that Spire Christian Comics published.

> While the adults sat out in the sun on the deck, eating bratwurst and potato chips, my sister and I stretched out inside, the heat magnified through the tall windows, paging madly through the comic books. We were seeking Archie comics, and more specifically Betty and Veronica. These two young women— it is no mystery, no big secret—they multiply heat. Wholesome Betty Cooper, with an endless supply of bikinis, prone to tying off her shirttails to reveal her stomach. And Veronica Lodge—so rich, and yet trashy enough to wear thigh-high vinyl boots. . . .
>
> The thick digests could hold us for half an hour, but by far the strangest and most titillating find were the Spire versions of Archie. Here, the whole gang in Riverdale was up to their usual hi-jinks, yet everything was evangelically inflected. It was as if the dialogue had been removed from a regular Archie and filled in with the New Testament. . . .
>
> "I've been reading Romans," Veronica said, slathering suntan oil over her long, slippery thighs.
>
> "As Jesus said: I am the way," Betty answered, a volleyball in one arm.
>
> I read on, transfixed, perplexed and excited by the combination of piety and raw sexuality.

Peter exaggerated only slightly. Those revised "Christian" *Archie* comics *were* embarrassing. I sensed that same holy discord in the booths with pink teddy bears who prayed the Lord's Prayer or in bumper stickers that proclaimed "Do you follow Jesus this closely?" and "This vehicle will be unmanned at the Rapture." I kept hearing Peter's wry wit as I considered what seemed incongruent with a majestic and holy God.

Was I immune to the temptations that come with recognition? Absolutely not! I did many radio and television interviews that week, and one afternoon I signed hundreds of copies of my newly released book *The Friendships of Women,* and a long line queued up. My ego inflated with thoughts of *Have I arrived? Am I really somebody in the Christian world?* My focus was blurring, changing my catechism to "The chief end of man is to enjoy Dee and glorify her forever."

The week ended with a church service on Sunday, beginning with a parade of one well-known gospel singer after another. Though there was no dry ice to simulate holy smoke, there was much cheering, clapping, and stomping of feet.

And then there was the moment everything changed.

R. C. Sproul walked out on the stage and began a convicting message: "The Holiness of God." Sproul described the prophet Isaiah's encounter with the Lord in the temple. The crowd hushed. We were brought to our senses as we remembered the extreme foolishness of all who try to profit themselves by using God, trifling with One who is absolutely pure and powerful. We had forgotten—and God used Sproul to remind us of God's holiness, His justice, and His severity.

## The Beginning of Wisdom

It was the same sense of fear and awe I experienced the day I knelt to surrender my life to Christ. For before He overwhelmed me with His love, He gave me a vision of just how self-centered, spoiled, and sinful I was.

I grew up protected and privileged, blessed with vaccinations and vacations, cared for and coddled as the baby in a family with three daughters. Jesus wasn't on my radar in childhood or early adulthood, so God sent a bolt of lightning to me in the form of my eldest sister, Sally.

Sally was a twenty-seven-year-old Spanish teacher at Iowa State who had just come to Christ through an essay one of her students had written. The assignment had been "Write an essay in Spanish on who your best friend is and why." A freshman by the name of Bonnie wrote an essay explaining why Jesus was her best friend. Sally was intrigued and began to invite Bonnie to babysit for her two little boys.

Each time Bonnie babysat, she left behind gospel tracts from Campus Crusade for Christ titled "The Four Spiritual Laws," which explained the gospel.

Sally says, "We found them everywhere—in the bathroom, in the kitchen—and my husband claims there was one under his pillow!"

Bonnie also began to ask Sally probing questions about Jesus. Then one night, when Sally took her home, Bonnie took a deep breath and asked, "Mrs. Frahm, have you seen those booklets I have left for you?"

"They were a little hard to miss."

"Did you read them?"

Sally pulled up to Bonnie's dorm and stopped. "Yes, Bonnie, I did."

Bonnie put her hand on the door handle and said rapidly, "Mrs. Frahm, is there any reason you couldn't give your life to Jesus Christ?" Then she opened the car door and bolted, her courage depleted.

That question haunted my sister until she surrendered to Christ. When she did, she would tell me later, "All things became new," just as we read in 2 Corinthians 5:17.

My stern and serious sister then decided she needed to visit me to tell me about how Jesus could change *my* life. She called me and asked if she could come to Indianapolis for a weekend to visit my new husband and me. Not knowing what was coming, I said, "I'd love to have you come!"

Upon her arrival, Sally pulled out a great big black Bible and started following me around the house, asking me hard questions about Jesus and quoting scriptures like "Do not be afraid of those who kill the body but cannot kill the soul. Rather, be afraid of the One who can destroy both soul and body in hell" (Matthew 10:28, NIV).

It was the longest weekend of my life. I tried to change the subject. I told her, "I'm lonely here—I haven't yet found a good woman friend."

Sally replied, "Jesus is my best friend."

I thought, *Good grief! I can't wait for her to go home!*

To my great dismay, a blizzard postponed my sister's departure for three days. Sally saw it as God's opportunity and continued haunting me. Yet, as the snow melted outside my window, my heart was softening as well. I pondered, *Was Jesus actually God? Am I a sinner? Am I in trouble if I don't surrender to Him?* I was undecided when my sister left, but now I could not rest until I knew the truth.

I read voraciously, including the Phillips New Testament my sister wisely left behind. The fear of God, which Solomon tells us is "the beginning of wisdom" (Proverbs

9:10), brought me to my knees. I was naked and vulnerable before the holy gaze of God, and I felt as Isaiah did when he said, "Woe is me! For I am lost; for I am a man of unclean lips" (Isaiah 6:5).

Certainly the biggest surprise in my twenty-two years of life was this moment when the presence of Christ was so real it made me tremble. I knew then without a shadow of a doubt that Jesus was not just one of many great teachers from the past but very God of very God. I was traumatized, given a heart wound, yet swiftly following this experience of the mysterium tremendum, God covered me with His amazing grace. As John Newton famously wrote, "'Twas grace that taught my heart to fear, and grace my fears relieved."

## Whatever Became of Sin?

There was a time when the Western world was not so healthy or wealthy and people came to church and hungrily read the Bible to understand their sorrow. They also accepted the biblical truth that the Christian God is a God of both love and justice. But today our Western world accepts only a God of love, shunning a God of holiness and justice.

In the movie *The Shack,* when God (played by the actress Octavia Spencer) was asked by Mack (played by Sam Worthington) about His wrath, the response was an incredulous "My what?"

Sam repeats: "Your wrath."

Olivia responds, "You lost me there."

This altered "god" is a creation of man. The true God *is* love, but He is simultaneously holy and just. The author of Hebrews describes Him as "a consuming fire" (Hebrews 12:29). It is His holy justice that demands a payment for sin, and it is His love that led Him to pay it in our stead.

In his classic *Whatever Became of Sin?* Karl Menninger noted how the word *sin* gradually became politically incorrect in the Western world. How different it was in Abraham Lincoln's day. In the midst of America's civil war, Lincoln saw that what America needed most was repentance and instituted the National Day of Prayer and Humiliation, explaining,

We have forgotten God. We have forgotten the gracious hand which preserved us
in peace . . . and we have vainly imagined, in the deceitfulness of our hearts, that

all these blessings were produced by some superior wisdom and virtue of our own. Intoxicated with unbroken success, we have become too self-sufficient to feel the necessity of redeeming and preserving grace. . . .

It behooves us then, to humble ourselves before the offended Power, to confess our national sins, and to pray for clemency and forgiveness.[1]

We don't hear this kind of prayer in politics today or even in many of our churches. Our prosperity has blinded us to our depravity and dimmed our hunger for God. God has been so gracious to America, but indeed He seems to be removing His protective hand, knowing that the time has come to allow severity to awaken us from our death sleep.

## I Did It My Way

The world loved the lyrics, made popular by Frank Sinatra, "I did it my way." But when we do it our way, we contract a virus that hurts us and spreads to others.

In the Garden of Eden, Satan implies to Eve that God does not have her best interests at heart and that instead of being her friend, He is her enemy. In truth, every time we sin, it is because *we do not trust the goodness of God,* so we endeavor to meet our needs our way.

Adam and Eve's sickness is evident immediately after they do it their way. Shame replaces joy, and so they hide. God, as the good teacher He is, asks Adam questions to help him own his sin.

"Where are you?" (Genesis 3:9).

Adam is hiding because he can no longer stand the holy gaze of God on his nakedness. (Nakedness in Scripture is symbolic of being fully seen.) Before they sinned, Adam and Eve were as innocent as children, but now everything has changed. Adam is no longer innocent, no longer unaware of his nakedness, and no longer joyful.

Adam answers God, "I heard the sound of you in the garden, and I was afraid, because I was naked, and I hid myself" (verse 10).

But it is not nakedness that is new. It is sin. So God asks another question. "Who told you that you were naked?" (verse 11).

Adam is silent. Now God is direct. "Have you eaten of the tree of which I commanded you not to eat?" (verse 11).

Adam admits he has, but he blames Eve and indirectly blames God, who gave her to him (verse 12).

Do you see? Three kinds of hiding are happening:

1. hiding from God by going behind the trees
2. hiding from themselves by making excuses
3. hiding from each other, by wearing fig leaves

Indeed, we all want to be covered. We don't want God or others to see us as we really are. But so often, instead of repenting and letting God wash us so that innocence can be restored, we grab a few flimsy fig leaves.

## Flimsy Fig Leaves

I am quite certain that at my funeral my son John will regale my friends with this story. He and his junior high friends once decided to skinny-dip in broad daylight at the lake near our cabin in Wisconsin. I heard their hysterical laughter on the shore and looked up to see boys with bare bottoms leaping into the water, leaving a pile of suits on their raft. Deciding they needed a lesson in modesty, I quietly motored out while they were frolicking in the water, grabbed the suits, and sped to shore to cries of

"Whoa!"

"Hey!"

"Mom—NOOOO!"

They swam in, endeavoring to stay covered by the water, doing the elbow crawl all the way up to shore. Then they crouched down and sprinted over the sharp stones, yelping in pain, trying to get to the cedar trees to grab branches to cover themselves.

Just as when we try to cover our sin, neither fig leaves nor cedar branches really do the job. Still we persist in grabbing them. How?

- We drop names or exaggerate our accomplishments, looking for approval from others instead of being content with God's approval.
- We don't practice hospitality because we want to hide our messy or humble homes, caring more about our images than ministering to others.
- We put on a religious front, even with our brothers and sisters in Christ, hesitating to tell them where we are failing and needing prayer.

We may even choose the fig leaf of "irreligion." Because the holy gaze of God is making us uncomfortable, we run the other way, deciding we don't believe in this God after all.

Tim Keller tells the story of a pastor who was preaching at a Christian college's chapel service. After the service, a freshman told him that he was narrow minded and that she didn't believe in this kind of God anymore.

After talking gently to her, the pastor discovered this young woman had grown up in a strong Christian home but had decided since coming to college that she didn't believe. He asked her when her belief had changed, and she told him "around Thanksgiving." He asked her if anything else had happened around Thanksgiving, and she admitted she had moved in with her boyfriend. The minister understood why sin didn't make sense to her—she couldn't stand the holy gaze of God.[2]

What happened to this young woman happens to many young people raised in evangelical homes who then go away to college, where cheap sex is everywhere. In an article in the *Washington Post,* Mark Regnerus backed this up statistically and wrote, "[Christian young people] want love, like nearly everyone else. They couple. Sex often follows, though sometimes after a longer period of time."[3] They then often begin to doubt God and turn away from church. "Cheap sex, it seems, has a way of deadening religious impulses."[4] When we get addicted to sin and do not want to repent, we also want to get out from under the holy gaze of God, so we grab the fig leaf of irreligion. But that doesn't work either. And neither do our vain attempts to cover our sin by ourselves.

So how can we be covered?

God is as kind as He is severe: "The LORD God made for Adam and for his wife garments of skins and clothed them" (Genesis 3:21). God is waiting to cover us, and His is the only covering that is effective. If we come to Him in true repentance, He will make us as white as snow.

## Paradise Lost and Found

Because of the Fall, the whole world changed. Sorrow, sickness, and death will come to every living thing. Indeed, this is the severity of God.

Recently as we were studying that Genesis 3 passage in a small group at our church, a visiting young Muslim woman from Turkey said, "I don't think it is fair that in your religion you have to suffer for Adam and Eve's sin."

I loved how Warren, a gentle and godly man, responded: "I don't like it either. And yet, when I look at my own heart, I know I would have rebelled too. It is human nature to sin, but God has not left us in our sin. He has sent a Rescuer in Jesus."

Our rescue is immediate, ongoing, and coming. We are rescued immediately from the penalty of sin when we put our trust in Christ. And though we have an ongoing battle with the power of sin, if we respond to His still small voice, we can be overcomers. And one day, all sin will be gone. We will be fully known (naked, so to speak) yet loved to the sky—this is the desire of every heart.

Already, here in Genesis 3, we glimpse the gospel.

God is speaking to the serpent (Satan): "I will put enmity between you and the woman, and between your offspring [seed] and her offspring; he shall bruise your head, and you shall bruise his heel" (verse 15).

In a patriarchal culture, "how significant," Derek Kidner comments, "was the passing over of Adam for *the woman* and *her seed.*"[5] The only woman who had a child without an earthly father is Mary, so "her seed" is Jesus. So not only will Satan and Jesus be in conflict, but their "seeds," or their children, will also be in conflict. Yet right after this ominous prophecy of two families at enmity with one another, we also have the promise of redemption.

Jesus will bruise Satan's head, and Satan shall bruise Jesus's heel. The word for "bruise" was a strong word in ancient times, not how we think of a bruise today. It is used in Isaiah 53:5 and translated "crushed," as "he was crushed for our iniquities." Though indeed Jesus was crushed at the cross, it backfired on Satan, for what Satan meant for evil turned out for good. Yes, Satan is still causing havoc and sorrow in this world, but there will be a final victory when he is thrown into the lake of fire forever. His crushing will be permanent (Revelation 20:10).

This promise of a good ending for our story is the melody of hope, played like a one-fingered tune on the piano in the books of Moses, soon to be joined by a full orchestra when we get to the Prophets. But it helps us understand the scope of the whole Bible to see that ever since the Fall, a war has been raging. We will now see the strategies God gives His children so that they can be victorious while living in enemy territory.

## Bible Study Three

As a group, view the related video and share comments: go to deebrestin.com and click on *The Jesus Who Surprises* under Free Teaching Videos. Also, as an option for going deeper, listen online to "Nakedness and the Holiness of God" by Tim Keller.

### Week Three God Hunt

We should always be looking for God to show up when we are with Him in His Word. Each day see if a verse becomes radioactive to you as you read that day's passage. If it does, slow down to discern what God might be saying to you. Continue also to be aware of His gifts during your everyday routines.

### Day One: Chapter Review

1. Read the chapter and highlight as you read. Write down two thoughts that particularly stood out to you.

2. If you listened to Tim Keller's sermon, share what stood out to you.

*Today I spied God when . . .*

### Day Two: The Liar and the Wonderful Counselor

3. Read Genesis 3:1–7.

   *a. In verse 1, what does Satan's question to Eve imply about God? Why do you think Satan wants to make that implication?

b. In verse 3, how does Eve add to what God said? Why do you think she does that?

*c. Think about the last time you sinned and then ask yourself, *What lie did I believe about God that caused me not to trust Him? What need was I trying to meet independently of Him?*

d. In what area of your life are you often tempted? How could you counteract the Enemy by speaking the truth to your soul at the time of temptation? How might you use Scripture? Give an example.

4. Read Genesis 3:8–13.

a. Write down a few things you observed about this passage.

b. Why is Adam's answer to God's first question faulty (see verses 9–10)?

5. In Genesis 3, what are the various ways that Adam and Eve try to hide?

6. Give an example of a time in your life when God convicted you using His Word. (Think of passages on forgiveness, marriage, money, parenting, or love.)

*Today I spied God when . . .*

## Day Three: The Battle and the Promise

7. Read Genesis 3:14–15.

   a. In verse 15, to whom is God speaking?

   *b. Who do you think is meant by "her offspring"? Why?

   c. Genesis 3:15 mentions a continuing battle between Satan's offspring and Christ's offspring. How do you see this battle continuing?

   d. The same word translated "bruise" or "strike" is used in Isaiah 53:5 and is translated "crushed." What insight does this give you into Genesis 3:15?

   *e. Why do you think verse 15 is called the first gospel?

*8. How does the Cross make it possible for God to be simultaneously loving and just? Kind and severe? (See 1 Peter 2:24.)

*Today I spied God when . . .*

## Day Four: Consequences for Woman, Man, and Marriage

9. Read Genesis 3:16.

   a. Whom is God addressing here, and what does He tell her?

   b. The word *desire* in verse 16 can mean both sexual desire and the desire to control (Genesis 4:7). Some think it is both, and it may be, but since sexual desire was there before the Fall, it seems the predominant emphasis is on control. In 3:16, how do you see strife entering the marriage relationship?

   *c. How could a husband or wife, through Christ, counteract this effect of the Fall? If you are married, have you experienced this power, this God sighting, in your marriage? If so, share an illustration.

10. Read Genesis 3:17–19.

    a. Adam is with Eve when Satan lied (see Genesis 3:6). How could he have helped? Why do you think he doesn't?

    b. What will happen to the ground, and how will this affect man?

    c. In what ways is your work a curse? In what ways is it a blessing?

    d. What is the final curse for all mankind, according to verse 19?

*Today I spied God when . . .*

## Day Five: One Day!

The last three chapters of Revelation show us a picture of the curse of Genesis 3 reversed, of the new heaven and new earth joined, of Eden redeemed. We will learn more about the new heaven and new earth in part 3 of this book, but for now let's just glimpse how this story will end.

11. Who is the serpent from the garden, according to Revelation 20:2?

12. What is in store for that serpent at the end of the story, according to Revelation 20:10?

13. Read Revelation 21:1–4 and share your comments, observations, and questions.

14. Who will live in this new place of beauty, according to Revelation 21:27?

15. Read Revelation 22:1–2. How is this new heaven and new earth reminiscent of Eden?

16. What is your takeaway this week and why?

*Today I spied God when . . .*

## Prayer Time

If your group is large, cluster in smaller groups of six or fewer. One of the most effective ways to pray is to use Scripture, for then you are praying within God's will, and He promises to answer those prayers. For example, this week we learned that Satan tries to make us think we can't trust God, so we are tempted to meet our needs independently of God. Look back at your answers under question 3d and formulate a request based on those observations about your own life. If you are willing, tell the group your request, along with any other urgent need you have.

# FOUR

# Crouching Tiger, Hidden Dragon

## *Overcoming Our Enemy in This World*

> The sin underneath all our sins is to trust the lie of the
> serpent that we cannot trust the love and grace of Christ
> and must take matters into our own hands.
>
> —MARTIN LUTHER

Our second son, John, is a bridge engineer who travels all over the world to oversee challenging bridge projects. Steve and I could tell early on that John was gifted with blocks, locks, and things mechanical. When John was two, we lived in a house on a cliff overlooking Lake Oswego, its clear blue waters surrounded by the green pine-filled hills of the Pacific Northwest. The cliff and the lake posed a real danger to our two curious little boys, so we screened in the porch on the back of the house and put swings, a slide, and a sandbox in the porch itself to serve as their "yard" in which they could safely play. Inside our house, we had only one door leading to the outside, and we added an extra bolt up high and always kept both locks locked.

Early one morning, Johnny climbed out of his crib, pushed the kitchen stool to the door, climbed up it, unlocked the bolt, unlocked the lower lock, and toddled outside in his footed PJs and soggy diaper.

When I found Johnny's crib empty and the front door ajar, fear seized me. I dashed outside, not even grabbing a robe to cover my nightgown, so desperate was I to rescue my son. I ran through the cul-de-sac yelling, "Johnny! Johnny! Johnny!"

Steve had already left to make early hospital rounds, so I pounded on neighbors' doors, gasping, "Please help me! Our two-year-old got out, and I can't find him!" Two men rushed down the steep wooden stairs to scan the lake. Others ran through the neighborhood, yelling, gathering others to join in the search. I cried out to God to protect our precious toddler. You can imagine my relief when I saw a neighbor many doors down climbing the hill into our cul-de-sac with Johnny on his shoulders.

My passion to find my son that day gives me a glimpse into the heart of God our Father and how He feels when His children—us—choose to believe the Enemy, open the forbidden door, and walk into immeasurable sorrow. Following this enemy could lead to our eternal death, and God's only thought is to rescue us from that danger.

As Philip Yancey writes, "In a nutshell, the Bible from Genesis 3 to Revelation 22 tells the story of a God reckless with desire to get his family back."[1] John tells us, "The reason the Son of God appeared was to destroy the works of the devil" (1 John 3:8).

We truly have an enemy, and we should not take him lightly.

## The Christmas Card You Never See

Christmas cards attempt to capture that first Christmas: the infant in a manger, awe-struck shepherds, the little town of Bethlehem. I have yet to see one depict the scene described in Revelation where Satan embodies not a slithering snake but a dragon, who stands before the woman who was about to give birth that "he might devour it" (12:4).

This is not a prophecy but a recapitulation of history. Satan wanted to destroy the infant Jesus and was behind Herod's slaughter of the male babies under the age of two. This passage also shows how Satan battled against Christianity in its infancy. Indeed, all the apostles except John were martyred. The emperor Nero covered many of the early Christians with hot tar and lit them on fire. But when they died trusting God, believing the best was yet to come, it only propelled the spread of Christianity. As the early church father Tertullian said, "The blood of the martyrs is the seed of the Church."

Though our enemy is cruel and powerful, we learn through Jesus *how* to overcome him. God put His first son, *the first Adam,* into a garden, and tested him—and he succumbed to the devil's lies. Then God's Spirit, at the beginning of Christ's ministry, drove the *second Adam* into the wilderness and tested Him. He overcame that same enemy, providing a model for us.

Our battle in this fallen world is not with flesh and blood but against "cosmic powers over this present darkness" (Ephesians 6:12). The first thing we absolutely have to realize is that we need help—we cannot overcome the Enemy simply by willing ourselves to stop our destructive behavior.

## We Can't Just Stop It

In a skit for *MADtv,* Bob Newhart plays a counselor advising a troubled young woman who is obsessed with fear about being buried alive in a box. He guarantees her that their counseling session will take less than five minutes and asks her to describe her problem.

Katherine explains, "I just . . . I start thinking about being buried alive and I begin to panic. . . . I mean I can't go through tunnels, or be in an elevator, or in a house—anything boxy." . . .

"All right, well, uh, let's go, Katherine. I'm going to, uh, say two words to you right now. I, uh, want you to listen to them very, very carefully. Then I want you to take them out of the office with you and in-incorporate them into your life. . . . You ready?"

She gets out her notepad and says, "Yes."

"Okay, h-here they are." He leans over his desk and yells at her, "Stop it!"

Taken aback, she stutters, "Sorry?"

He shouts, "STOP IT!"

Confused and fearful, she repeats, "Stop it?" . . .

"You know, it's funny. I-I-I say two simple words and I cannot tell you the amount of people who say exactly the same thing that you're saying. . . . This is not Yiddish, Katherine."

When she starts to explain how this fear began in childhood, he holds his hand up: "We—we don't go there—just, just stop it."[2]

But we can't just stop it. In fact, if we try, our obsession grows, like those tiny sponge dinosaurs children drop in water that swell into monsters. That is because while God's law is good and clearly defines sin, when we or someone else tells us not to do something, the sin in us, Romans 7:8 explains, turns it into a "piece of 'forbidden fruit'" (MSG).

So what shall we do? I'm eager to share what so many Christians are discovering to be a powerful Spirit-led strategy against our enemy.

## First: Ask God to Help You See the Sin Beneath the Sin

One of the biggest surprises from Jesus that I have had in the last ten years is His revealing to me the sin beneath my sin. In the past, instead of looking at *why* I was engaging in destructive behaviors, such as eating too much sugar, spending too much, or indulging in too much anxiety, I just scolded myself, slapped my hand, and said, "Bad Dee! Stop it!" But that only made me want to eat, spend, and worry more.

The captain of the *Titanic* saw the head of the iceberg but underestimated the massive body of it beneath the water. In the same way, we are prone to attack the visible aspects of our sin and ignore the hidden causes. We try a new diet, a new budget, or a new anger-management plan and wonder why none of these produce lasting results. To use another metaphor, it is because we've simply chopped the head off the dandelion instead of digging out the root. What is the root? It is always idolatry. Instead of trusting God, as Jesus always did, we run to false lovers, as Gomer did in the book of Hosea. Instead of casting our burdens on Him, we run to food, friends, or Facebook. Instead of trusting His love, we crave the fleeting praise of others. We think these false lovers are the ones who will actually help us. Sometimes it isn't until those idols turn on us and bring us pain that we are willing to go to the Great Physician or to the body of Christ for help.

Often we can identify the bad fruit coming out of our lives, but it may be hard to see what hidden idol is causing it. One day in Bible study my dear friend Ann H. made herself vulnerable. She said, "I need help. My visible sin is that I am extremely judgmental and critical of others. I have been convicted by His Spirit that this is wrong, but I can't seem to stop. So here is my question: What is my heart idol? What need am I trying to meet through this sin that Jesus could meet instead?"

Sylvia jumped in. "Ann, I so identify, because that is one of my big temptations. I have come to realize through prayer and the counsel of others that my heart idol is approval. I want others to think I would never do the things these 'bad people' are doing."

Ann nodded. "That makes sense, because I am particularly critical of Christians who are behaving badly. They embarrass me. And I really don't want others to think that I would do those things too, since I'm a Christian too."

This is a small group at its best—with iron sharpening iron. Sylvia helped Ann recognize her sin beneath the sin—she was looking for approval from man instead of being content with approval from God. This was the first step leading to victory. So the next question is, How do we replace this heart idol with God?

### Second: Speak the Truth of the Gospel to Your Soul

In that study, I asked, "So, Sylvia, at the moment you are tempted to think or speak critical thoughts to gain man's approval, what do you do about it?"

"First," she said, "I have to speak the gospel truth to myself: that though I may not be bad in the way the person I am criticizing is bad, I am bad in other ways—in fact, I am so bad that Christ had to die for me. But then, I have to reflect on His love for me. Dee, remember that poem you quoted from John Donne when he asked God to ravish him?"

I smiled and quoted the closing of "Batter My Heart":

Except you enthrall me, never shall be free,
nor ever chaste, except you ravish me.

"Yes! I need to remind myself, indeed, to melt my heart with Christ's love. He loved me enough to go all the way to the cross for me, and now, because of that, I am cleansed and beautiful in God's eyes. He loves me just as much as He loves His Son—and I don't have to do anything to earn it, because, as Jesus said at the cross, 'It is finished.' When I meditate on that at the time of temptation, it helps me to give more grace to the person I am thinking critically of and it meets my need for approval so I'm not so desperate to have the approval of others."

Sylvia was following the model Jesus gave us when He was tempted in the wilderness. Again and again Satan tries to make Jesus think that God will not meet His needs. This is how Satan succeeded with Adam and Eve, so he tries the same tactic with the second Adam. The second Adam, unlike the well-fed first Adam, has been fasting for forty days, so He is particularly vulnerable. Satan slithers in to imply that God isn't caring for Jesus, so He'd better care for Himself. Satan says, "If you are the Son of God, command these stones to become loaves of bread" (Matthew 4:3).

Do you see the lie? God isn't caring for you, isn't providing food for you, so turn these stones into bread.

The lie is *always* an attack on God's being sufficient to meet our needs. Jesus *knows* His Father cares for Him, so He replaces the lie with the truth: "It is written, 'Man shall not live by bread alone, but by every word that comes from the mouth of God'" (verse 4). There is something more important than physical food. Here Jesus takes us back to

Moses when the Israelites are complaining about the manna God has given them to eat. They are craving the leeks, garlic, and cucumbers they had in Egypt so much that they want to go back! They are forgetting the bricks, the beatings, and the bondage of Egypt.

Moses tries to get them to replace the lie with the truth that "man does not live by bread [or garlic and leeks] alone" (Deuteronomy 8:3). God has given them freedom from slavery, which should mean more to them than their menu.

We have such deceitful hearts that we are willing to go back into slavery rather than release our heart idols. Implicit in every temptation is the deception that God doesn't really care for us, so we must take matters into our own hands. Again, we must remind our souls that He cares for us. We can speak the gospel to our hearts, and we can also remember the times in the past when He *has* cared for us.

I think back on the many times since Steve died that God came to my rescue when I cried out to Him to "be my husband." One memory in particular comes to mind.

The driveway to my cabin in Wisconsin is a long, steep hill that goes down through the forest. In the winter it is often snow covered. Though the driveway was slick one morning, I thought, *I think my Subaru can handle this.* I got a running start, but midway up the hill, my Subaru stalled, swerved, slid backward into the woods, and stopped, stuck in the snow, just before it plowed into a giant cedar tree.

Shaken but unhurt, I got out, praying, "Oh Lord, You promised to be a husband to the widow. I need You to be my husband right now." At that moment, Jonathan Orrick, a godly man in my church, happened to be driving on the highway that passes my neighborhood. After he passed, he had the strong impression *Go check on Dee.* Though wondering, as we often do, if he had really heard from God, he turned around and came to my driveway. As I was retreating carefully down the icy driveway to my cabin, I heard the rumble of a truck at the top. I turned around only to see—Jonathan! *How in the world?*

I cried, "Jonathan! How did you know I needed you?"

Shaking his head in amazement, he said, "I sensed I should check on you." Then God gave Jonathan the skill and the wisdom to coax that little Subaru out of the woods and all the way to the top of my driveway.

We have a Father in heaven who will provide for us as He does for the lilies of the field (Matthew 6:28). We are told, "Just as you trusted Christ to save you, trust him, too, for each day's problems" (Colossians 2:6, TLB). But Satan is a liar and the Father of Lies.

He says we cannot count on God to care for us. Spotting this lie every time we are tempted can make us overcomers.

### Third: Play the Whole Tape Through

A large percentage of prison inmates have been addicted to drug or alcohol. They started using because they thought those things would help them in some way. The program Celebrate Recovery, which is a Christian version of Alcoholics Anonymous, encourages participants to "play the whole tape through." When they desire to return to drugs, it is because they know drugs will make them feel great. But if they play the whole tape through, they know that will be followed by bondage and destruction. This is true anytime we run to an idol. At first, idols seem to be our friends, but after they give us momentary relief, they turn on us, cutting us to pieces.

In *The Missing Piece*, Lee Ezell writes, "I've learned that often the wrong decision seems easier at first, but leads to great pain later and the right decision seems harder at first, but leads to great peace later."[3] Ezell's life story is such an illustration of this principle, for she was tempted to abort the child she conceived through rape. Indeed, that *seemed* like a merciful solution for Lee. But Lee thought ahead to what her life would be like in the future if she aborted this child and decided she couldn't live with that decision. She listened and responded to God's whisper and gave birth to a daughter, whom she gave up for adoption. Julie turned out to be the only child Lee was ever able to conceive, and when Julie became an adult, she and Lee were reunited. Oh, the joy they found, for Julie is the image of her beautiful and godly mother and a voice for the voiceless babies conceived through rape.

We may think the commandments of God are hard, and indeed they can be initially, but every single commandment He gives us springs from His deep love for us and leads to peace in the long run.

Once a woman who helped clean my house stole some emerald jewelry that Steve had given me. After she got out of jail, the Lord allowed me to lead her to Christ. She was so thankful to be freed from the penalty of sin, but she asked, "Can the Lord also free me from my sticky fingers?"

"Yes! He's the only One who can!" I explained to her that the sin beneath her stealing was idolatry. Instead of trusting God to provide for her through honest work and trusting Him, she had resorted to her own sinful way. And yes, stealing had provided for her momentarily, but then it had turned around and cut her to pieces. Since idols cannot be removed, only replaced, she *couldn't* just stop it. She needed to trust the love of God to provide for her. This is turning from fig leaves to faith. It's been ten years, and she has stayed clean and God has met her needs His way: her honest work and His surprising provisions.

What causes a person to commit adultery? Instead of trusting God to meet his (or her) needs for love or sexual satisfaction, he goes after another man's wife. Again, there is momentary pleasure, but then he is destroyed. And again, he can't just stop lusting; he must ask his loving God to meet his needs within marriage or give him contentment as a single man. Again, moving from fig leaves to faith.

Satan tells those who are tempted that they won't be happy unless they go outside God's boundaries. Wesley Hill, who struggles with same-sex attraction but has chosen to live a celibate life, says he knew the devil was crouching at the door waiting to over-power him, but he chose not to believe Satan's lie that he couldn't be happy living celi-bate. Hill gives strong testimony in the great joy he has found in trusting God with this struggle:

> [This] conviction . . . has become the heartbeat of my life—that we gay Chris-tians, in the words of C. S. Lewis, can actually be "a real ingredient in the divine happiness." We can please God, can truly experience his pleasure in the midst of sexual brokenness, and in the end can share in his glory.[4]

Quite honestly, it is a surprise to find the joy that Jesus gives when we resist tempta-tion. We are expecting pain, and though we might experience that initially in saying no to our heart idols, what follows is such an amazing joy that it helps us find more strength to resist Satan the next time. This is why we find admonitions against idolatry through-out the whole Bible.

## "Little Children, Keep Yourselves from Idols"

I have always loved John's first letter, but it wasn't until I memorized it that I saw that idolatry is its theme.

All the way through 1 John, the apostle warns against our enemy, the devil. And then he closes his letter with, "Little children, keep yourselves from idols" (5:21). He hasn't mentioned idolatry once in his letter, so that closing seems to come out of the blue. But idolatry is the sin beneath the sin in every sin he has been addressing throughout the whole letter. The reason we fail to walk in the light or hold to the truth or love our brother is because of idolatry, the sin beneath the sin.

John gives a specific example from Genesis when he says,

> This is the message that you have heard from the beginning, that we should love one another. We should not be like Cain, who was of the evil one and murdered his brother. And why did he murder him? Because his own deeds were evil and his brother's righteous.
> —1 John 3:11–12

So what was Cain's idol? I suspect, like for his parents, it was control. He wanted to be in control instead of God. God had accepted Abel's offering but not Cain's *not* because it was a blood sacrifice rather than grain (grain offerings were acceptable according to Leviticus 2) but because something evil was going on in Cain's heart.

God comes to Cain gently, for He knows what he is plotting, and tells him to do what is right—to repent of his jealousy. He wants to help Cain see this for himself, so just as He did with Adam, He asks questions: "Why are you angry, and why has your face fallen? If you do well, will you not be accepted? And if you do not do well, sin is crouching at the door. Its desire is contrary to you, but you must rule over it" (Genesis 4:6–7). But Cain digs in his heels, determined to take the reins from God and solve this problem another way than repentance. He would just get rid of his brother. This was a temporary solution that led to enormous pain. God had painted a word picture for him of sin being like a crouching tiger that "desired" to have Cain. The Hebrew word translated "desire" means the desire to control. The picture of the White Witch in Narnia is apt. As soon as Edmund takes the witch's Turkish Delight, he becomes her slave. We sin because we are deceived, thinking that sin is our friend.

Cain refuses to repent, and indeed the tiger pounces. Yet, amazingly, God is *for* us, even when we sin. Even after Cain murders Abel, God gives him a chance to repent. He comes to Cain and asks, "Where is Abel your brother?" (verse 9). God's question is not to get information but to help Cain confess.

But Cain responds, "I do not know; am I my brother's keeper?" (verse 9).

Fig leaves.

Since Cain was unwilling to repent and run to God, now all that is left is God's holy justice:

> The LORD said, "What have you done? The voice of your brother's blood is crying to me from the ground. And now you are cursed from the ground, which has opened its mouth to receive your brother's blood from your hand. When you work the ground, it shall no longer yield to you its strength. You shall be a fugitive and a wanderer on the earth."
>
> —verses 10–12

Cain says this is more than he can bear. Indeed, sin is never our friend.

## A Better Word

The author of Hebrews also refers to Cain but emphasizes how this story is a picture of the gospel rescue. Do you remember how Cain's blood from the ground cried out to God for justice? In the same way, Christ's blood calls out for justice for us, and this, Hebrews says, is "a better word" (12:24).

Have you ever thought, *How many times can God forgive me for the same sin?* I have! Even though I've known the Lord for so much of my life, and now I am definitely in my third act, I don't have my act all together. I fail Him every day in thought, word, and deed. It would be easy to despair if I believed His patience could run out and He might say, "Enough! Dee has had enough time, and she's still failing!"

But the truth is, each time I come to God in genuine repentance, the blood of Jesus my Savior cries out to God from the ground, cleansing me from all unrighteousness. My forgiveness is not based on my ability to get it together but on the blood of Christ.

Ever since Cain and Abel, there have been two families in conflict. I remember when our firstborn, JR, brought up this truth as only a four-year-old can! We had invited new neighbors for dinner. Halfway through our meal, JR piped up.

JR: "Do you guys love Jesus?"

Uncomfortable pause.

JR: "Uh-oh. Do you love the devil?"

Uncomfortable laughter.

Neighbor: "Ah, JR, are those our only choices?"

I don't remember how we got out of that one, but I remember thinking, *Yes, those are your only choices.*

John's first letter makes it very clear that we are either a child of Satan or a child of God:

> No one born of God makes a practice of sinning, for God's seed abides in him;
> and he cannot keep on sinning, because he has been born of God.
>     —3:9

> By this it is evident who are the children of God, and who are the children of the
> devil: whoever does not practice righteousness is not of God, nor is the one who
> does not love his brother.
>     —3:10

The battle between these two families—the children of the devil and the children of God—continues all the way through Scripture.

You might think the war is between those who outright deny Christ and those who profess Christ, but that isn't where the primary battle is at all. As we'll see in the next chapter, throughout Scripture, God keeps showing us two sons, two paths, two identities. Both, like Cain and Abel, profess faith in God, yet only one has genuine faith.

## Bible Study Four

As a group, view the related video and share comments: go to deebrestin.com and click on *The Jesus Who Surprises* under Free Teaching Videos. Also, as an option for going deeper, listen online to "Worshiping Idols Without Knowing It," a twelve-minute interview with Dee Brestin.

### Week Four God Hunt

In addition to noticing daily gifts and radioactive verses, be alert so that you can recognize the sin beneath the sin this week. Often our bodies give us clues that an idol is at work: we are tense, angry, anxious, sad . . . At that point, ask yourself, *Why am I downcast [or angry, or nervous . . .]? Where am I not trusting God?* Then talk to your soul about why you *can* trust God—and surrender. If you see progress, give the credit to God in your recordings of "Today I spied God when . . ."

## Day One: Chapter Review

1. Read the chapter and highlight as you read. Write down two thoughts that impressed you and share at least one with the group.

2. For those who watched the interview with Dee Brestin, do you have comments?

*Today I spied God when . . .*

## Day Two: The Battle with the Second Adam

Tim Keller writes that "[God said to Adam], 'Obey me about the Tree and I will bless you'—and Adam didn't do it. But to the second Adam he says, 'Obey me about the Tree" [the cross] 'and I will crush you'—and Jesus does."[5]

3. Read Matthew 4:1–6.

   a. According to verse 1, who leads Jesus into the wilderness and why?

   b. God also tests Israel in the wilderness. Why do you think God does this? (Psalm 66:10 and Hosea 2:15–17 provide a hint.)

    c. What is the lie Satan is trying to get Jesus to believe with his first temptation?

    d. How does Jesus overcome this lie?

4. Read Luke 22:1–6 and then explain who was behind Judas's betrayal. What did he hope to accomplish?

5. Read 1 Corinthians 15:3–4 and explain how Satan's plan backfired.

6. Read 1 Corinthians 15:45–49. What promise is here?

*Today I spied God when . . .*

## Day Three: The Sin Beneath the Sin

7. Think about an area of your life in which you struggle with temptation. Have you tried to just "stop it"? What has been the result?

8. How might you speak the truth about God to your soul and to Satan when you are facing the temptation you identified? Be specific.

9. What insight do the following verses give into why just trying to stop a sin often backfires?

> The law code started out as an excellent piece of work. What happened, though, was that sin found a way to pervert the command into a temptation, making a piece of "forbidden fruit" out of it. The law code, instead of being used to guide me, was used to seduce me.
> —Romans 7:8–10, MSG

10. Read Exodus 20:1–3.

    a. How does God preface the Ten Commandments in verses 1–2? Why do you think that is?

    b. How has trusting God brought you out of slavery? Give a specific example of a sin that enslaved you and describe how God has brought or is bringing you out.

*c. What is the first commandment? Explain why obeying this would help you to obey all the rest. Give one illustration.

*Today I spied God when . . .*

## Day Four: Cain: A Case Study in Idolatry

*11. All through his first letter, John has been exhorting believers to walk in the light, to walk in love, and to walk in truth. How does he close his letter (5:21)? Why, do you think?

*12. Read 1 John 3:8–15.

a. According to verse 8, if someone makes a practice of sinning, what does it reveal?

b. And why, according to verse 9?

c. What are two characteristics of the children of the devil, according to verse 10?

d. Why did Cain murder his brother, according to verse 12?

13. Read Genesis 4:1–7.

   a. When anything bad comes out of our lives, we can know that a
      heart idol is operating. In verse 5, what do you see in Cain?

   *b. On the basis of verses 3–5, what heart idol might have been
       operating in Cain? (A heart idol is a need God wants to meet,
       but because we don't trust Him, we find our own sinful way of
       trying to meet that need. It could be comfort, control, approval,
       among others.)

   c. What encouragement does God give Cain to let Him fill that need
      (verse 7)?

   d. What does God warn Cain about if he tries to fill his need his own
      way (verse 7)?

   e. Using the word picture in the second sentence of verse 7, how might
      you speak to your soul the next time you are tempted with one of
      your besetting sins?

*Today I spied God when . . .*

## Day Five: A Better Blood Than the Blood of Abel

14. Read Genesis 4:8–16.

    a. How does sin overpower Cain in verse 8? What light does 1 John 3:12–15 add?

    b. How do you see God giving Cain a chance to own his sin in Genesis 4:9? And how does Cain respond in that same verse?

    c. What does God tell Cain in verses 10–12? How does this show that God cared about Abel and will be just? Does this help you not to take vengeance into your own hands? Why or why not?

    d. How does Cain show remorse in verses 13–14? How is this different from repentance?

    e. In verse 15, do you see God's mercy toward Cain despite the hardness of his heart?

f. What happens to Cain in verse 16?

g. Some people say, "I can't believe in a God who sends people to hell."
   What insight does this passage give regarding who chooses hell?

15. Read Hebrews 12:22–24. What blood "speaks a better word than the blood of
    Abel"? What does this mean? (Refer to the close of chapter 4 if you need to.)
    Be still before the Lord and let Him search you so that you may confess and
    truly repent of any known sin.

16. How might you apply this lesson to your life right now?

*Today I spied God when . . .*

## Prayer Time

If your group is large, cluster in smaller groups of six or fewer. In addition to one personal need you might have, turn your answer to question 7 or 15 into a prayer request.
Then the facilitator will lift up each person's name and you can pray brief sentence
prayers. When there is a pause, he or she will lift up the next person's name. You might
get ready by writing your request here.

# FIVE

# Religion Versus the Gospel

## *From Obligation to Grateful Joy*

It is not enough to claim Abraham as our father.
The crucial question concerns who our mother is.

—JOHN STOTT

Before Ron and Debbie put their trust in Christ, I sensed God was moving in their lives, shaking up the thoughts they had held for so long. Both had tried to be good people. Ron had worked with Habitat for Humanity, while Debbie had ministered to the elderly. Both had been churchgoers. Yet when Debbie came to a retreat I was giving, she sensed something was missing from her life. She asked me, "Why can't I stop crying when you speak?"

I told her, "I think God is wooing you."

She cried again. "I think He is!"

Debbie began coming to our seeker's study on *Examining the Claims of Jesus,* and then she'd go home and tell Ron all about it. I decided it was time to invite Ron and Debbie over for dinner in what turned out to be a most "Jesus Surprising Day."

We were clearing the dishes when Ron startled me by pounding on the counter with his big fist, saying, "What you've been teaching my wife is not what I've heard in church all my life!"

I froze. "How is it different, Ron?"

"You told her all she has to do is put her trust in what Jesus did at the cross and she'll go to heaven."

"That's right."

He leaned forward and glared at me with his piercing blue eyes: "So she doesn't have to be good?"

"Oh, Ron—wait—I want to show you something." I ran and got Tim Keller's *Gospel in Life* from my bookshelf and then laid it open to show Ron this chart:[1]

Ron furrowed his forehead and read through the chart while I waited in silent prayer. Then that big blustering man revealed his beautiful heart by humbly saying, "I guess I'm religious. So now what do I do?"

In the months to come, God rescued both Debbie and Ron from religion and

| Religion | Gospel |
| --- | --- |
| "I obey; therefore, I'm accepted." | "I'm accepted; therefore, I obey." |
| Motivation is based on fear and insecurity. | Motivation is based on grateful joy. |
| I obey God in order to get things from God. | I obey God to get God—to delight in and resemble him. |
| When circumstances in my life go wrong, I am angry at God or myself, since I believe that anyone who is good deserves a comfortable life. | When circumstances in my life go wrong, I struggle, but I know all my punishment fell on Jesus and that while God may allow this for my training, he will exercise his Fatherly love within my trial. |
| When I am criticized, I am furious or devastated, because it is critical that I think of myself as a "good person." Threats to that self-image must be destroyed at all costs. | When I am criticized, I struggle, but it is not essential for me to think of myself as a "good person." My identity is not built on my record or my performance but on God's love for me in Christ. |
| My prayer life consists largely of petition, and it only heats up when I am in a time of need. My main purpose in prayer is control of the environment. | My prayer life consists of generous stretches of praise and adoration. My main purpose is fellowship with God. |
| My self-view swings between two poles. If and when I am living up to my standards, I feel confident, but then I am prone to be proud and unsympathetic to failing people. If and when I am not living up to standards, I feel humble but not confident—I feel like a failure. | My self-view is not based on my moral achievement. In Christ I am simul iustus et peccator—simultaneously sinful and lost, yet accepted in Christ. I am so bad that he had to die for me, and I am so loved that he was glad to die for me. This leads me to deep humility and confidence at the same time. |
| My identity and self-worth are based mainly on how hard I work, or how moral I am—and so I must look down on those I perceive as lazy or immoral. | My identity and self-worth are centered on the one who died for me. I am saved by sheer grace, so I can't look down on those who believe or practice something different from me. Only by grace am I what I am. |

brought them into the freedom of the gospel, replacing their strivings with peace. Later Ron told me, "In all my seventy-three years, I never knew such joy was possible."

Reviewing the Religion Versus the Gospel chart is a good way to determine where your trust is. Even true sons tend to revert to religion, but if you find yourself on the left side of the chart more than on the right, I pray you have the tender heart Ron had and cry out to God to rescue you from yourself.

## Two Sons, Two Ways of Approaching God

Abraham had two sons, one representing the way of religion and one the way of the gospel. God had promised Abraham a son, but as Sarah aged past childbearing years, the couple took things into their own hands. At Sarah's request, Abraham slept with Sarah's handmaiden, Hagar, to bear a son (Ishmael) through her. Later, God allowed Sarah to conceive a son supernaturally (Isaac).

Paul uses this story as an allegory to represent two ways of approaching God. Galatians 4:24 states, "These women are two covenants." This allegory is complicated but beautiful. Hang in there with me! Once you get this, you will understand the whole scope of the Bible! As John Stott says, "An understanding of the Bible is impossible without an understanding of the two covenants."[2]

Our whole Bible is divided into two covenants: the Old Testament, representing the Old Covenant, the way of the law and religion; and the New Testament, representing the New Covenant, the way of grace and the gospel.

On the outside, these two sons may look similar, but oh, how different are their hearts. One has a morally restrained heart and the other has a supernaturally changed heart. Likewise, their eternal destinies are radically different, for to the first, Jesus will say, "I never knew you" (Matthew 7:23).

The physician and theologian D. Martyn Lloyd-Jones observed in a sermon that the way a person responds if you ask him if he is a Christian tells you if he is trusting in himself (religion—with a morally restrained heart) or in God (the gospel—with a supernaturally changed heart). If he gets miffed that you would even ask, he interprets your question as an accusation that he is immoral. But if he responds with joyful glee, with something like "Yes—isn't it wonderful?" then he understands that his salvation has absolutely nothing to do with his own righteousness.[3]

Once when ice-skating with a new friend in Fargo, North Dakota, I wanted to find out where she really was with Jesus, for though I knew she was a churchgoer, I had never heard her speak of the Lord in a personal way. I decided to probe with what I hoped was a gentle question. I asked, "Would you say that you are a Christian, or that you are still on the way?"

Oh, how that backfired on me! She exploded in anger, "Miss Dee, why would you think I am *not* a Christian? What is so bad about me?" She was so angry, she couldn't hear me as I stuttered to explain that I wasn't saying anything about her being good or bad—I just wondered if she'd been able to trust what Jesus did for her. She skated off the rink in a huff and hobbled down to the locker room with her skates still on, wanting to get far from me! I've never tried that evangelistic tactic again.

That is a lot like the reaction Jesus receives when He tells the Pharisees that if they knew the truth, they would be set free. They explode, "We are offspring of Abraham and have never been enslaved to anyone. How is it that you say, 'You will become free'?" (John 8:33).

But Jesus, instead of backing up, persists, for He can see their hearts. He tells them they are not free but slaves, enslaved by religious rituals and outward appearances. The argument escalates with Jesus telling them, "You are of your father the devil" (verse 44).

They are certain they are the true sons of Abraham. They accuse Jesus of having a demon and ask, "Are you greater than our father Abraham, who died?" (verse 53).

Jesus absolutely dumbfounds the Pharisees when He responds to their question: "Before Abraham was, I am" (verse 58).

In the Greek, the word translated as "I AM" is a double evocative, the very same expression that God spoke to Moses when He declared, "I AM WHO I AM" (Exodus 3:14). For God is above all and cannot be compared to anyone. *I AM* is always a declaration of deity.

The Pharisees pick up stones to throw at Him, for when you see the *real* Jesus, you either want to be rid of Him or fall on your knees and worship Him.

## Who Is Your Mother?

In truth, these Pharisees *were* sons of Abraham. But Abraham had two sons. What matters, John Stott explains, is who your mother is: Hagar or Sarah?[4]

Hagar's story represents an attempt to save ourselves independently of God. When Abraham and Sarah fail to believe the promise that God will rescue them through

Sarah supernaturally conceiving a son by Abraham, they come up with their own natural plan.

This is the way of the law, of religion, of man. "Sons of Hagar" represent those who think they need to rescue themselves but cannot because they are too weak. Indeed, the purpose of the law, Paul tells us, is to lead us to Christ, to show us we *can't* do it and must fall on His mercy. If we refuse to do so, we will be like the religious Pharisees whose hearts produced the fruit of depression, pride, anger, and all the things listed under the religion column in the Religion Versus the Gospel chart (see page 70).

But Sarah's miraculous story represents letting God rescue us, trusting His promise. This leads to the good fruit of humility, joy, peace, and all the things listed under the gospel column in the chart.

Likewise, Hagar's son Ishmael and Sarah's son Isaac represent the two peoples who descend from Abraham: the false and the true, the slave and the free, the Old Jerusalem (the Jews who are religious but do not embrace the gospel) and the New Jerusalem (true believers, the invisible church, both Messianic Jews and believing Gentiles who embrace the gospel).

Hagar was a slave, so her son Ishmael was as well. Doing it our own way or trusting in the idol of religion makes us slaves. That's what Jesus keeps telling the Pharisees that makes them so angry. They feel that all the rules and rituals they have kept should make them right with God. They are claiming Abraham as their father, which he is—but the slave woman, Hagar, is their mother.

Jesus wants to set those Pharisees free from their slavery, but, for the most part, they will not listen. Remember how Jesus weeps over Jerusalem, saying, "O Jerusalem, Jerusalem, the city that kills the prophets and stones those who are sent to it! How often would I have gathered your children together as a hen gathers her brood under her wings, and you were not willing!" (Matthew 23:37).

Those of us who do believe, who have embraced the gospel, can also sometimes default to religion and lose the joy and peace we have in Christ, becoming slaves to performance again. Martin Luther observed, "Even after you are converted by the gospel, your heart will go back to operating on the religious principle unless you deliberately, repeatedly set it to gospel-mode."[5]

When my husband died of cancer in his fifties, I often found myself in despair, thinking, *I deserve this. I'm such an idiot. I fail God all the time.* During one of those days when I was beating myself up, I was listening to a sermon and the preacher said,

"When a Christian suffers, it is *never* because God is punishing him, because Jesus paid it all at the cross, and it is finished." I thought, *I knew that*. My train had jumped the gospel track, but the truth helped me set my heart back to the gospel mode.

You will need to set your heart back to the gospel mode often. When you are anxious, downcast, or angry, do what the psalmist did and speak to your soul:

> Why are you cast down, O my soul,
> and why are you in turmoil within me?
> Hope in God; for I shall again praise him,
> my salvation and my God.
> —Psalm 42:11

Stop trusting in yourself and get back on the gospel track.

## False Sons Will Persecute True Sons

These two sons, Ishmael and Isaac, have a rocky relationship. On the day Isaac is weaned, they have a great feast, and Sarah sees Ishmael mocking Isaac. This foreshadows the battle that would continue between their descendants.

Just as Ishmael mocked and persecuted his half brother Isaac, so do our "half brothers" mock and persecute us. John Stott explains that most of our persecution comes not from the world but from

> our half brothers, religious people, the nominal church. It has always been so.
> The Lord Jesus was bitterly opposed, rejected, mocked and condemned by His
> own nation. The fiercest opponents of the apostle Paul, who dogged his footsteps
> and stirred up strife against him, were the official church, the Jews. . . . And the
> greatest enemies of the evangelical faith today are not unbelievers, who when
> they hear the gospel often embrace it, but the church, the establishment, the
> hierarchy. Isaac is always mocked and persecuted by Ishmael.[6]

The hardest speaking engagement I had in all my decades of speaking was to a group of women ministers from a liberal denomination that no longer embraced the gospel. They called themselves Christians because they exhorted their congregations to obey the golden rule of loving their neighbor, yet they shunned the real Jesus, the Cross, the blood sacrifice, and the claim that He and only He is "the way, and the truth, and the life."

One good test of gospel-centered preaching is that your sermons might cause you to be thrown in jail or even martyred in countries hostile to Christianity. The pablum these preachers were serving from their pulpits would not even raise an eyebrow.

Why was I invited to be the main speaker at their retreat? The women felt that my book *The Friendships of Women* provided a "safe" topic and would help them love one another.

I saw the invitation as an opportunity to present the gospel. I began with my testimony and immediately sensed hostility. At the first break I was taken aside by the head of the committee and told, "We are paying you to speak about friendship. Get back on track."

I admit I was shaken, but I knew before God that I could not change my talks and strip Jesus and His gospel from scriptural friendships. Indeed, you cannot authentically tell the story of Ruth and Naomi without showing how this story foreshadows Christ and His plan of redemption, redeeming us not with silver and gold, as Boaz did for Ruth and Naomi, but with His precious blood. When I said that, I saw women roll their eyes at one another. *The blood. How archaic.*

At lunch, after my morning session, I carried my lunch tray to a table of women, and though there were empty seats, they told me they were taken. I tried another table. The same. So I sat down at an empty table and no one joined me. I ate quickly and escaped to my book table, but only two women bought books. Then they tucked them in their bags and hurried off, eager for no one to see what they had done.

After lunch, fewer than half the women returned to the lecture hall. I was being boycotted. I spoke of the friendship of David and Jonathan and explained how Jonathan, who laid down his life for his friend, points to Christ. And when I closed with the friendship of Mary and Elizabeth to usher in the greatest event of history, the birth of our Savior, who was the only way we could be rescued from the deserved wrath of God, some got up and walked out.

After the session I packed up my books, alone, carried them to the car, alone, and cried all the way home. I was so eager to get to Steve and have him comfort me, which he did. He reminded me that if they persecuted Jesus, they would persecute me. He said he suspected that a few there might be pondering what I'd said and seek out the truth, as Nicodemus had. Steve said I probably wouldn't know until heaven what fruit came from this event, but he was confident there would be some, for God's Word does not return void. Steve urged me to pray for these ministers, for only God can breathe life into those who are dead, only God can remove the blinders. And I do pray, for I grieve that these false shepherds, like the Pharisees of old, are leading their flocks to trust in religion instead of the glorious gospel.

Before we leave this section and sail into the poetry of the Psalms, we will look at a story that not only runs through the rest of the books of Moses but is indeed the plotline of the Bible. I'm excited to begin the story of our family—how Jesus does not just surprise us but astonishes us.

## Bible Study Five

As a group, view the related video and share comments: go to deebrestin.com and click on *The Jesus Who Surprises* under Free Teaching Videos. Also, as an option for going deeper, listen online to "The Prodigal Sons" by Tim Keller.

### Week Five God Hunt

This week, be alert to how the gospel can set you free on a daily basis: your identity, your response to criticism or trials, your security concerning God's love. Continue being alert for other ways of spying God as well and record those God sightings each day.

### Day One: Chapter Review

    1. Read the chapter and highlight as you read. Write down two thoughts that impressed you and share one with the group.

2. For those who listened to Tim Keller, what did you learn?

*Today I spied God when . . .*

## Day Two: Religion Versus the Gospel

3. If someone you didn't know well asked you if you were a Christian, would you be offended? Why or why not? How would you respond?

4. Look at the first three items on the Religion Versus the Gospel chart. On which side do you tend to fall?

*5. Look at the fourth item in the chart concerning when circumstances in your life go wrong. The book of Job shows us a righteous man who suffered greatly—and his three friends were sure it was due to sin. Read 4:6–7 and find the lies of this "religious" man, Eliphaz.

6. All through the book of Job, his friends assume that his suffering is due to sin. How does God make it clear in 42:7–8 that Job's suffering is *not* due to sin?

7. Martin Luther said that "religion" is our default mode. We tend to slip back into it. Looking at the last four items on the chart, where do you tend to slip back into religious thinking?

*Today I spied God when . . .*

## Day Three: Two Sons of Abraham

8. Read John 8:31–38 and find some differences between the religious one and the one the Son has set free.

9. Describe how the argument intensifies in verses 39–47.

10. Read verses 48–58 aloud. What comments and observations do you have?

*11. According to verses 31–58, how do you think Jesus would contrast the difference between religious identity and gospel identity?

12. Did any of the verses from this week's readings in Job or John become radioactive to you? If so, which one(s) and why?

13. Read Genesis 16:1–4 and describe what happened.

14. Read Genesis 17:15–19 and describe God's promise.

15. Read Galatians 4:21–26 to see how Paul uses this historical story as an allegory. Think in terms of how working independently of God produces barrenness in many ways and how submitting to Him produces fruitfulness.

    a. According to verse 23, what is the primary difference between the son of the slave woman and the son of the free woman?

    b. How do religious people try to make themselves right through the flesh? What was the result for Abraham? Sarah? Hagar?

    c. The Jerusalem of this world is in strife, but the New Jerusalem coming down from heaven to be on earth will be filled with children of peace, born of the promise. What is the primary difference between these two cities, according to verses 25–26?

*d. Explain how religion enslaves but the gospel sets us free. Give one specific illustration, if possible, from your own life.

*Today I spied God when . . .*

## Day Four: Two Ways of Approaching God

Religion always wants to add just a little to the gospel: "Trust Jesus plus _____, then I will be right with God." The Judaizers tell the Galatians to trust Jesus, plus be circumcised and follow the law, and then they would be approved.

16. Read Galatians 1:6–10.

   a. What is Paul's tone and message in verses 6–9?

   b. In what ways do you see churches today turning away from the gospel message? Why do you think that is?

   c. According to verse 10, what does religion try to do, and what does the gospel do?

17. Read Genesis 15:1–6.

   a. What question does Abram ask, and what promise does God give him?

   b. How does Abram respond?

18. Read Romans 4:1–12 and explain how Paul uses this account of Abraham as an illustration of a gospel-centered response.

19. Read Genesis 16:1–6.

   a. Who do you think Abram was trying to please here?

   b. How is this an illustration of the religious response?

   c. How did this lead to slavery for all of them?

*Today I spied God when . . .*

## Day Five: Two Identities

20. In biblical days and (to some degree) today, a woman's identity is often tied to her ability to bear children. That is how she gets approval from man. How does Paul turn this on its head by quoting Isaiah 54:1 in Galatians 4:27?

21. When we trust that because of Jesus we are already approved, we may be freed to make choices that are not necessarily valued by the world. Give some examples of this.

22. Have you been freed to do this? Explain.

23. What is your takeaway this week and why?

*Today I spied God when . . .*

## Prayer Time

Using conversational prayer, begin with thanksgiving for ways you sensed Jesus at work in your life this week. Then each person will lift up a personal request of his or her own in prayer and allow the others to lend support with sentence prayers.

# SIX

# The Plotline of the Bible

## *The Story of the Lamb*

Behold, the Lamb of God, who takes away the
sin of the world!

—JOHN 1:29

God knew He was going to call my husband and the father of our five children home in his prime, before all his children were grown, but we surely didn't. We were oblivious to the hurricane that was gathering strength and headed toward us.

Instead, our focus was our firstborn daughter, Sally (named after my sister Sally), who had come home to heal after going through great sorrow while living in Kraków, Poland. Sally expressed her pain at her easel, producing painting after painting of menacing darkness, expressing the sorrow that had shaken her world and saturated her very being. As she painted she lamented to God, as the psalmists teach us to do. In time, shafts of light began to filter into Sally's paintings.

Living in Kraków had made Sally acutely aware that she was not alone in her pain. She visited the death camp of Auschwitz, with its ovens and its memories of a living hell. She often walked through the old Jewish quarter. She said that though it was beautiful, it felt haunted, holding the memory of Jews who had been herded there before being transported to the death camps. Some of those people were relatives of Sally's Jewish grandmother Brestin, who escaped Poland as a teenager but had to leave behind many from her own family. In light of her own losses and the tragedies of history, Sally pondered the age-old question *How could a good God allow such evil and suffering?*

When she returned to the States, Sally went to Covenant Seminary in hopes of finding healing answers. In addition to taking Bible courses, she studied the mysterious relationship between faith and art.

One book that had a profound impact on her during this time was Madeleine L'Engle's *Walking on Water: Reflections on Faith and Art.* Though L'Engle has often been controversial in the evangelical world, Sally knew I respected her as a true believer whose unconventionality stirred healthy discussions.

In *Walking on Water,* L'Engle writes about what she learned from Hawaiian Christians, who would sit before the Lord listening so that they might "breathe life" into their prayers. The Hawaiians had a name for the Caucasians on the Island: *haoles,* meaning "without breath." They looked so white that they reminded the Hawaiians of corpses.

The Hawaiian Christians began to also notice that many of these Christian haoles also lacked breath in their prayers. They prayed briefly and perfunctorily. In contrast, the Hawaiians would meditate over Scripture and endeavor to be still and listen to the Lord before they prayed, so that *He* could fill their prayers with breath and truth. For L'Engle, meditating, listening to God, and breathing life into her prayers before she wrote was vital.[1]

L'Engle told a story that illustrated how the Spirit of God could give a manuscript or a work of art a life of its own. It happened when she was writing *The Arm of the Starfish* and a character she had not planned suddenly appeared in the story. Her protagonist, Adam, woke up one morning after being plunged into a deep sleep, and there, sitting in a chair looking at him, was Joshua.

In *Walking on Water,* L'Engle writes, "Adam was very surprised to see Joshua. Madeleine was even more surprised to see Joshua. There had been no Joshua in my plot at all."[2]

But now he was there, and L'Engle had to rewrite 150 pages to accommodate him. It turned out he was a Christ figure, and indeed the name Joshua means Jesus. Madeleine had not intended to put a Christ figure in, but there he was. She could have refused him entry into the story, but she wanted to have faith in the creative process and the God to whom she had breathed her prayers.[3] All this was to affect Sally profoundly and influence her art—which would lead to a "lamb" we would never forget.

## "Who Said Anything About Safe?"

The summer after Sally's year at Covenant, she was still wrestling with the question of suffering. Inspired by L'Engle, she decided she would ask the Lord to reveal His answer through her art. Every morning she went to the little studio above our garage to paint. Before she painted, she sat before the Lord, listening, meditating, and breathing life into her prayers. She felt led to paint a portrait of Aslan, the Christ figure in the Chronicles of Narnia series by C. S. Lewis.

As a little girl Sally had always loved Narnia, especially the scene where the children first heard about Aslan, "the Lord of the whole wood":

> "Is he a man?" asked Lucy.
>
> "Aslan a man!" said Mr. Beaver sternly. "Certainly not! I tell you he is the King of the wood and the son of the great Emperor-beyond-the-Sea. Don't you know who is the King of Beasts? Aslan is a lion—*the* Lion, the great Lion."
>
> "Oooh," said Susan, "I'd thought he was a man. Is he—quite safe?" . . .
>
> "Safe?" said Mr. Beaver. . . . "Who said anything about safe? 'Course he isn't safe. But he's good. He's the King, I tell you."[4]

Sally asked God to help her paint the paradox: a Lion who was not safe but was good. She explained,

> I first constructed canvas that was bigger than any art store could sell me, because Aslan needed to be big. I wanted him stepping down into the viewer's space, like you couldn't get away from him. So I thought, Okay, I'm going to lay my canvas down and take this really thick, like, modeling paste, this textural matter, and I'm going to throw it down to bring about the structure of Aslan's body from what just kind of happens spontaneously. Better said, let the Lord construct and teach me and tell me what to do.[5]

For two weeks, Sally worked hard on the painting but couldn't get the paradox— she couldn't paint a lion that was both "not safe" yet good. She started all over. This time she came down from her studio and said, "I've got the 'not safe' part, but I still can't get the 'good' part." She was frustrated, but she didn't give up, for the Lord had impressed on her heart, *This is a special painting, Sally. You've got to get this one right.* When she had a peace that she had done all she could, she stopped, though she still couldn't see the "good" part of Aslan.

After Sally put the painting on display at our church, a woman we didn't know came up to her and said, "Sally, do you see the other animal in this painting?"

Sally shook her head, thinking of how people see all kinds of things in abstract art. Then the woman stepped up to the massive painting and reached high to outline a good-sized lamb with her finger. His body was hidden in the lion's dark mane, his legs masked by the gold-and-brown-flecked background of the painting.

Suddenly Sally saw it: a lamb who looked as though his legs were bound—a lamb who looked like he had been slain. She froze, chills going up and down her spine: the mysterium tremendum. She thought of John's vision in the book of Revelation of "the Lion of the tribe of Judah" (Revelation 5:5). When John looked again, he saw a lamb who "had been slain" (verse 6).

Though this still wasn't an answer as to *why* God allows suffering, it shows what the answer is *not*. It is *not* that He doesn't love us, for He is the Lamb of God who was willingly slain for our sins.

Nor is the answer that God has lost control. At the close of Job, God speaks to Job out of a whirlwind and points to the stars, the seasons, and the splendor of all His creation to show Job He knows what He is doing. On this earth, all we, with our finite minds, need to know is that He loves us and is in control. As someone has said, when we get to heaven and no longer see "through a glass, darkly" (1 Corinthians 13:12, KJV), we will simply say, "Of course."

Just weeks after the lamb was revealed in Sally's painting, the hurricane of Steve's fatal diagnosis hit. We were anticipating a long-awaited family vacation with our three youngest children. First, Sally and Annie were accompanying me to a retreat where I was speaking in Indianapolis. Then we planned to drive to our cottage in Wisconsin and meet up with Steve and our daughter Beth. Steve had been having stomach problems and decided to get checked for an ulcer before they left. He called me just hours before I was to speak. It wasn't an ulcer; it was advanced cancer. Fourteen months later our beloved husband and father would be with Jesus.

As Steve was taking his last breaths, it tore my heart to hear Sally cry, "Daddy— don't leave me!" Yet God knew the storm ahead and gave us the miraculous painting of Aslan. It *has* comforted us, and not just us, for prints and posters of this painting now hang in prison cells, hospital rooms, funeral parlors, and homes across the world. The massive original now hangs in the foyer of the Marion E. Wade Center at Wheaton College in Illinois. This is a museum that holds collections from seven British authors, including C. S. Lewis. God was comforting not just Sally but also thousands of His children in this world full of trouble. (In the accompanying video to this chapter's Bible study, you will see the painting and Sally telling the story.)

## From the Creation of the World

As wonderful as our own personal story of the lamb appearing in Sally's painting is, it is nothing compared to the wonder of seeing that the story of the Lamb is the plotline of the Bible, from Genesis to Revelation.

Indeed, the *same* gospel runs through both the Old and the New Testaments. Tim Keller tells of how in his early twenties, before he went to seminary, he "had held the vague, unexamined impression that in the Old Testament people were saved through obeying a host of detailed laws but that today we were freely forgiven and accepted by faith."[6] But then he heard the Old Testament scholar Dr. J. Alec Motyer speak and was "thunderstruck"[7] when Motyer asked them to imagine how the Israelites under Moses might have given their testimony of faith. He said they would have said something like this:

> We were in a foreign land, in bondage, under the sentence of death. But our mediator—the one who stands between us and God—came to us with the promise of deliverance. We trusted in the promises of God, took shelter under the blood of the lamb, and he led us out. Now we are on the way to the Promised Land. We are not there yet, of course, but we have the law to guide us, and through blood sacrifice we also have his presence in our midst. So he will stay with us until we get to our true country, our everlasting home.[8]

Dr. Motyer concluded, "Now think about it. A Christian today could say the same thing, almost word for word."[9]

The blood of innocent lambs spills throughout the pages of the Old Testament but ceases when John the Baptist heralds Jesus as the Lamb of God. Jesus is the only Lamb who can take away our sins (Hebrews 10:4, 10). All the other sacrificial lambs were simply a foreshadowing of the One to come. In fact, Revelation tells us about the "Lamb that was slain from the creation of the world" (13:8, NIV). It is as if time does not exist for God—it has always been faith in this Lamb that saves us.

## Why Does God Test and Try Us?

When those Old Testament believers put their faith in God, they were putting their faith in the Lamb that had not yet been fully revealed to them. Even so, God was foreshadowing Him again and again. That foreshadowing begins in Genesis, when God tests Abraham with a most mysterious command: "Take your son, your only son Isaac, whom you love, and go to the land of Moriah, and offer him there as a burnt offering on one of the mountains of which I shall tell you" (22:2).

Every person God has used mightily has gone through some kind of fire, beginning with Abraham, the father of all believers to come. God has already asked Abraham to send away Ishmael, his son with his bondservant, and that tore Abraham's heart. Now this? How mystifying, for God not only has repeatedly forbidden child sacrifice, though it is very common among other nations (Leviticus 20:2–3; Deuteronomy 12:31), but He has promised Abraham that from Isaac will come as many descendants as stars in the sky.

How can Abraham obey God's terrible command and simultaneously believe the promise? The author of Hebrews tells us that Abraham reasoned that God could raise the dead (11:19). Can you even imagine having that kind of faith?

So Abraham and Isaac go to the mountain. In *The Jesus Storybook Bible,* Jago, the illustrator, shows the "only son" Isaac carrying the wood for the sacrifice on his back up the mountain as a clear foreshadowing of another "only Son" carrying the cross on His back up the mountain to be the sacrifice.

God never intends Isaac to be sacrificed, but Abraham does not know that. So he lays Isaac on the wood and raises his knife. Then an angel stays Abraham's hand, a ram is caught in the thicket, and Abraham names the place of the miracle "the LORD will provide" (Genesis 22:14).

We have to get out of our narrow cultural mind-set to fathom this story. In our culture, the individual's happiness is preeminent, and families and communities are sacrificed on the altar of individualism. But that has never been God's way—and in most cultures and for all centuries, the reverse was true. Individuals willingly sacrificed themselves for the good of the family and the community. For example, there was a time when abortion, euthanasia, and divorce were rare, because people made personal sacrifices to care for the family. Today it's much more common for the unborn, the elderly, and the vulnerable to be sacrificed on altars of individual freedom. Abraham was willing to sacrifice his own son for the sake of following God, but God rescued him by offering to sacrifice *His* Son for the sake of all of us.

Perhaps the most striking foreshadowing of the Lamb of God occurs in Exodus. Pharaoh refuses to let Israel, God's firstborn son, go, saying, "Who is the LORD, that I should obey his voice and let Israel go? I do not know the LORD, and moreover, I will not let Israel go" (5:2).

God's wrath falls on Pharaoh and the Egyptians through the plagues, but still, Pharaoh will not listen. So God tells Moses that there will be a final plague, the death of every firstborn son from Pharaoh to the slave girl to the cattle. Moses tells the Israelites that their firstborn sons will die as well unless they apply the blood of a lamb without blemish to the doorposts of their homes.

What a picture of what we must do to be spared from God's judgment. Jesus is the perfect Lamb of God, without blemish, and He willingly sacrificed Himself for us. If we trust in His blood, the justified wrath of God will pass over us.

At the Last Supper, Jesus gave His disciples bread, saying, "'Take, eat; this is my body.' And he took a cup, and when he had given thanks he gave it to them, saying, 'Drink of it, all of you, for this is my blood of the covenant, which is poured out for many for the forgiveness of sins'" (Matthew 26:26–28). Truly, this is the Passover we who are in union with Christ are to keep, speaking the gospel to ourselves every time we take communion, for indeed—from creation to the end of time—the blood of the perfect Lamb of God has rescued us.

## From Head to Heart

When you read the books of Moses with the spectacles of the gospel—and indeed all the books of history and law this section represents, from Genesis to Esther—you cannot help but see that the Bible isn't about us but about Jesus. Jesus is the greater Adam, who resists the temptation that felled the first Adam. Jesus is the greater Isaac, who is sacrificed for our sin. Jesus is the greater Moses, who leads His people out of slavery and into the Promised Land. And Jesus is the great sacrificial lamb, the perfect Lamb of God, who takes away the sin of the world.

When you read the Psalms and the whole section of poetry that the Psalms represents, from Job through the Song of Songs, you again see Jesus and His gospel foreshadowed. But the books of poetry have a peculiar power. While the books of history and law appeal to our minds, the books of poetry, rife with emotion and multi-faceted metaphors, penetrate our very hearts.

They say the longest distance is the eighteen inches between the head and the heart. It is one thing to repeat the truth that Jesus is our Redeemer; it is quite another to *know* the presence of that Redeemer on a daily basis.

We've learned how the story began, how it went wrong, and how God planned our rescue from the start. Now let us continue on to the Psalms and learn how to *live* in this story.

## Bible Study Six

As a group, view the related video and share comments: go to deebrestin.com and click on *The Jesus Who Surprises* under Free Teaching Videos. Also, as an option for going deeper, listen online to "The Story of the Lamb" by Tim Keller and "Is He Worthy?" by Andrew Peterson.

### Week Six God Hunt

God helped Madeleine L'Engle write, helps Sally Brestin paint, and helps His children to do His work in the world every day. Be alert to how He helps you to serve Him. And continue to be alert for other ways you spy Him, recording those moments below under "Today I spied God when . . ."

### Day One: Chapter Review

1. Read the chapter and highlight as you read. Write down two thoughts that impressed you and share one with the group.

2. If you listened to "The Story of the Lamb" by Tim Keller, what do you remember and why?

*Today I spied God when . . .*

## Day Two: The Purpose of Testing and Trying Our Hearts

3. Read 1 Peter 1:3–9 aloud and share your comments and observations.

4. Can you think of a believer, in your small group or in your life, who faced a trial with trust? How did that impact you?

5. Read 2 Corinthians 5:7–12 aloud and share your comments and observations.

6. Read 2 Corinthians 5:16–18 and explain what will help us overcome trials.

7. Have you faced a trial that helped you know your faith was genuine? If so, explain.

*Today I spied God when . . .*

## Day Three: Father, Where Is the Lamb?

8. Read Genesis 22:1: "After these things God tested Abraham." What had happened in 21:8–14 that would increase the severity of this test?

9. Read Genesis 22:1–5 aloud.

   a. Share your comments and observations.

   b. What does God ask of Abraham in verse 2, and how is this verse a foreshadowing of what God would ask of Himself?

   c. How does Abraham respond in verse 3?

   d. What is the significance of "the third day" (verse 4)?

   e. What does verse 5 reveal about Abraham's thinking? How is this supported by Hebrews 11:17–19? What comments do you have on his faith?

10. Read Genesis 22:6–19.

    a. Who carried the wood up the mountain for the sacrifice in verse 6? Compare this to John 19:16–17. What do you see?

    b. What question does Isaac ask, and how does Abraham answer in Genesis 22:7–8? How was this a prophetic answer (verse 13)?

    c. What does Abraham name the place (verse 14)?

    d. Describe a time when God provided for you.

11. Do you think that in our culture the family's and the community's health take a back seat to individual freedom? If so, how? How should we respond as believers?

*Today I spied God when . . .*

## Day Four: When I See the Blood, I Will Pass over You

12. Read Exodus 12:1–13.

   a. Describe what the lamb was to be like (verse 5) and when it would be killed (verse 6).

   b. What were the Israelites to do with the blood and why?

   c. Describe what this night must have been like for everyone—the sounds, the smells, the emotions. How does this foreshadow a time to come?

   d. In the midst of terror, God protected those under the blood of the Lamb. Can you share a God Hunt of a time God protected you amid frightening circumstances?

13. Read Exodus 12:24–27 and describe God's command.

14. Read Matthew 26:26–29 aloud.

    a. Share your comments and observations.

    b. Describe what Jesus says at this Passover remembrance.

    c. Matthew does not tell us how the disciples react. What do you
       imagine they are thinking?

    d. Why is this now the ceremony we are to keep?

15. Read John 19:32–36 and find the parallel with the Passover lamb in Exodus
    12:46.

16. Read Matthew 27:45–46 and find the parallel with the Passover lamb in
    Exodus 12:6.

*Today I spied God when . . .*

## Day Five: Reading the Bible with the Spectacles of the Gospel

17. As you review what we've covered from the books of Moses, what are some ways you saw the gospel foreshadowed?

18. What are some ways you saw Jesus foreshadowed?

19. Does this strengthen your faith in the validity of Scripture? Why or why not?

*Today I spied God when . . .*

## Prayer Time

Rather than giving prayer requests, with eyes open but still praying, begin by giving thanks for some of the tender mercies you recorded this week. Then, when there is a pause, each person will share his or her personal request and allow the request to be supported by a few sentences from others. When there is another pause, another person should share a request, and so on.

# PART TWO

# How to Live in the Story

## *The Psalms*

# SEVEN

# The Surprising Way to Pray

## Authenticity as the Path to Intimacy with God

> If You won't give me back my wife, give me peace! Give me peace! . . . I'm confused! I'm mad! I love You, Lord, I love You, but I am mad at You! I am mad at You!
>
> —SONNY, praying in the movie *The Apostle*

When my granddaughter Miabelle was a baby, I gave her a little slice of mango. She tasted the smooth sweet flesh tentatively with her tongue, her eyes widened in delight, and she laughed out loud. Then she began to suck, making happy noises, throwing her head back and closing her eyes in ecstasy. But her mother, who feared nearly toothless Miabelle might choke, took the mango from Mia's little hand. Shocked, Mia's eyes flooded with tears, and then she collapsed on the floor, sobbing in utter despair.

Brennan Manning, in *Abba's Child,* included a chapter titled "The Pharisee and the Child,"[1] in which he highlighted the differences between Pharisees and children and explored why Jesus tells us to become like little children. The child is utterly unconcerned with appearances. Is she hungry, scared, disappointed? She wails! Is she pleased, delighted? She laughs, jumps, and claps her hands. The Pharisee pretends everything is fine, for he is focused on gaining adulation for himself, and therefore appearance is everything. The Pharisee acts as if he does not need help. The child knows she does and looks to her parent for every need. And Jesus says, "I tell you the truth, unless you change and become like little children, you will never enter the kingdom of heaven" (Matthew 18:3, NIV).

We might hesitate to tell a holy God what we are actually feeling, especially when we are angry or disappointed with Him, but He *shows* us through the prayers of lament what is not only permissible but also wise. It's silly to hide our thoughts from God, for He knows them already and it pleases Him when we are honest, inviting Him to speak into our situations.

I have a friend whose daughter, whom I will call "Lily," recently gave birth to her second child. When she brought her newborn home, her husband told her, "Two is too many." He packed his bags and abandoned his family. Brokenhearted and weary, Lily told her mother, "I am so angry at God."

My friend wisely said, "Tell Him. Tell Him exactly what you are feeling. Tell God how angry you are."

This was the best way to counsel Lily, for what Satan wants to do is cause *attachment disorder* between God and us. This is a term used to describe children who have trouble attaching to anyone because of abuse in their formative years. Satan wants to convince us that God does not love us and does not want the best for us so that we will back away and stop talking to Him, throwing away our only lifeline.

Let's consider how the Old Testament poets prayed. We will be strengthened to be genuine as we see how their prayers led them to experience the presence of God.

## The Prayers in the Book of Job

Job was the first to model the lament for us, for though he is placed in the poetry section of the Old Testament, he actually lived during the time of Genesis. Consider how boldly honest Job was in his prayers:

> I cry to you for help and you do not answer me;
>> I stand, and you only look at me.
> You have turned cruel to me;
>> with the might of your hand you persecute me.
> —Job 30:20–21

Job's life is full of sorrow not because of sin but because Satan is stalking him. So Job laments, and God comes to Job three different times and reveals transforming truth to Job. The poetry of Job excels any book on suffering you will ever read. It ministered to me when I was in high-tide grief, for Job felt what I felt and showed me how to keep talking to God, even when I was angry and confused by Him. I also could see Jesus as the greater Job, for He was a man acquainted with grief and able to empathize with my sorrow.

## The Prayers in the Song of Songs

Just as Job models lament in the first book of the poetry section of Scripture, the last book in the poetry section, the Song of Songs, models a degree of passion that makes many uncomfortable. Could it really be that God would use the marriage bed as a metaphor for how He rejoices over us as a bridegroom rejoices over His bride? Yes! (See Song of Songs 4; Isaiah 62:5.)

Some feel it simply cannot be, and therefore the Song of Songs must be only a book about the beauty of marriage. Yet we know from Ephesians 5:31–32 that marriage foreshadows the deeper mystery of Christ and His bride. There is so much evidence for Christ being hidden in the bridegroom in the Song, but I've already written a book about that (*He Calls You Beautiful*), so for here I will simply say that the Song is another story of rescue that illustrates the power of the gospel. This bridegroom takes the bride from a place of shame (Song of Songs 1:6) to a place of confident joy, where she is dancing between two armies (Song of Songs 6:13)! The Song of Songs is *not* an exception to what Jesus tells the two on the road to Emmaus—that He and His gospel rescue are hidden in *all* of the Old Testament.

When I first began to see Jesus hidden in the bridegroom in the Song of Songs, I melted to think that Jesus could love me like *this*. I began to use the Song as a springboard for both praise and petition. I tell Him that He is the fairest of ten thousand (5:10), that He "is altogether lovely" (5:16, NIV), and how much it means to me that, despite my sin, He sees me as beautiful (4:7) and His "banner over me [is] love" (2:4). Boldly I ask Him to "kiss me with the kisses of his mouth" (1:2). And as I am alert, He does surprise me with His kisses: seeing a double rainbow after a storm, a verse becoming radioactive, or the sense of His pleasure, like oil flowing over me, when I choose the narrow path so that nothing comes between me and my Lord.

## The Prayers of the Psalms

The poets penetrate our hearts with their authenticity and word pictures, and though I wish we could look at every poetic book of the Old Testament, we cannot. So we are going to camp primarily in Psalms in part 2 not only because they are the "psalms" Jesus mentions on the road to Emmaus but also because they show us, better than any other book, how to stay close to God no matter what life brings. William Brown writes, "Rife with the pathos of praise and the ethos of agony, the book of Psalms captures better than any other corpus of Scripture the 'bi-polar' life of faith."[2]

But to understand the psalms, we must understand how they are unique. Philip Yancey says he had been told to go to the psalms for comfort, but then he would come across one of the wintriest psalms and go away "frostily depressed."[3] How comforting, for example, is this?

> Your wrath has swept over me;
>     your dreadful assaults destroy me.
> They surround me like a flood all day long;
>     they close in on me together.
> You have caused my beloved and my friend to shun me;
>     my companions have become darkness.
> —Psalm 88:16–18

But then Yancey realized that while all the other books in the Bible are written from God to us, the psalms are written from God's children to Him.[4] They are inspired, but it is as if we are reading over the shoulder of David and the other psalmists as they journal their prayers.

At times the psalmist is thankful, remembering to praise the Lord for His many benefits. Other times he is angry and disappointed with God and tells Him so! Usually, in those psalms of lament, the psalmist reaches a resolution by the close of the psalm, for laments often lead to God reminding us of *why* He can be trusted, and the psalmist, by the close, does exactly that. But a few psalms simply end in despair, as does this one:

> Look away from me, that I may smile again,
>     before I depart and am no more!
> —Psalm 39:13

Can we really talk to a holy God like this? Yes! Derek Kidner's comment on Psalm 39 has brought great comfort to me: "The very presence of such prayers in

Scripture is a witness to his understanding. He knows how men speak when they are desperate."[5]

How I love this! He made us, He knows us, and He longs for honest communication. Intimacy is possible *only* when pretense is gone.

Think about what makes Jesus so angry over and over again—it is the pretense and dishonesty of the Pharisees. He is *not* angry with Job, Naomi, the prophets, or the psalmists who lament, and indeed He often comes running to them. But He is angry with the Pharisees. They put up a facade, a wall that keeps them from experiencing intimacy with the Lord, and one day He may surprise them by saying, "I never knew you; depart from me" (Matthew 7:23).

The Psalms model that authenticity. I'd like to spend time now plumbing the depths of my favorite psalm, a short but potent poem that helps us live victoriously in a fallen world.

## "Our Mouth Was Filled with Laughter"

Psalm 126 begins with the psalmist remembering a time of delirious happiness and relief:

> When the Lord restored the fortunes of Zion,
>     we were like those who dream.
> Then our mouth was filled with laughter,
>     and our tongue with shouts of joy;
> then they said among the nations,
>     "The Lord has done great things for them."
> The Lord has done great things for us;
>     we are glad.
>     —verses 1–3

You might think, from the opening lines, that the psalmist is in a joyful time, but that is *not* the case, for in his prayer, in the next part of the psalm, he pleads with God to restore the fortunes of His people. They are in a time of great trouble, so to buoy his soul as waves crash over them, he recalls another time of trouble when God reversed their fortune, rescued them, and filled their mouths with laughter.

We can't be sure what this wonderful thing was—only that there was a great deliverance. It could have been the Exodus from Egypt. Matthew Henry thinks it might have been the release from Babylon; Derek Kidner thinks the agricultural images portray a time when God dramatically rescued them from a famine. In any case, it was a time when God astounded His people by turning their sorrow into joy. It was a time they could *never* forget.

This is why I have been asking you to do a God Hunt every week as you read this book: we draw closer to God as we remember what He has done for us. And as we remember what He has done in the past, we begin to see what He is doing today.

I am so thankful that Karen and David Mains, authors and radio hosts, introduced our family to the God Hunt, for we had a reservoir of memories of God's faithfulness to sustain us all when Steve died.

We began our God Hunt when our oldest children started school. We hung a big bulletin board next to our family supper table to post God sightings through words or artwork. We continued this for at least fifteen years as our family grew. The Mainses gave us four specific ways we could spy God:

1. Any obvious answer to prayer
2. Any unexpected evidence of his care
3. Any help to do God's work in the world
4. Any unusual linkage or timing[6]

Most of the time the children's sightings were tremors (a snow day, new shoes, fun at recess), but occasionally they were earthquakes that jolted us with the reality of God. Some of those earthquakes that our children remembered and that correspond with the Mainses' categories were

1. Our springer spaniel, who ran off during a lightning storm, and for whom JR and Johnny fervently prayed for days, was found and returned safe and sound! (An answer to prayer.)
2. A friend stood up to the third grader who'd been teasing Annie about the shape of her eyes, and the bullying stopped! (Evidence of His care.)
3. Sally and her teenage friends received surprising permission from the public high school principal to show *The Jesus Film* in the auditorium on a Saturday during Lent. (Help to do His work in the world.)

4. When Beth was turning ten, she gave up hope of ever being adopted. Just
then she was told a family had been found for her—us! (Unusual timing.)

Recording and retelling increases memory—memory that is sorely needed in times
of trouble. At times, for our family, the appearance of God was *so* astounding that our
mouths were filled with laughter (Psalm 126:2) and at others we sat up and said, "The
LORD has done great things for them" (also verse 2). One such instance, a story we have
told and retold, is the birth of our daughter Sally.

## A God Hunt We'll Never Forget

Steve and I had been blessed with two sons, who were nine and six. I had an overwhelming desire to have a daughter, and I was so ready to try. But when I told Steve, he felt
differently. He felt our plates were full and we shouldn't take on more. He also reminded
me there was certainly no guarantee that we would have a girl. In fact, it was more probable now, statistically, that we would have a boy.

I told him I knew that and I would rejoice over another son but that we could ask
God for a daughter, because perhaps God had put that desire in my heart.

Steve was silent and finally suggested we both pray. He was leaving in the morning
for a three-day medical convention. As we had done before when we disagreed, we
agreed to surrender our own desires (as much as possible, considering the deceitfulness
of our hearts) and ask God to show us His desire and thus make us like minded.

During those three days, I endeavored to surrender my will, but my desire for another baby only seemed to strengthen. I had an idea. I thought, *What if I stop using
birth control for three months? If I don't get pregnant during that time, I will trust that
our quiver is only meant to hold two arrows and I'll go back on birth control.* (I know
some Christians believe birth control is wrong. Birth control is one of those gray areas
in Scripture, and Romans 14:1–12 urges us not to judge our brother but to be fully
persuaded in our own minds, for we will each individually give an account to God.)

When Steve came home from the convention, we sat down. He began, "My heart
hasn't changed, but I don't know if that is God's will or just a lack of faith in taking on
another child. But here is my idea: What if you stop using birth control for three months?
If God gives us a child, I will trust Him, but if He does not, would you be willing to
trust that it is not His plan and go back on birth control?"

My heart leaped! Surely God had given us the same idea, the same mind, because

He was going to answer my prayer for a daughter! Excitedly, I bought a pink baby book and asked Steve to help me be specific in prayer, suggesting we write down our requests so that we would have a record should God be so merciful.

So we made this list, telling the Lord that if He had a better idea, He should trump our ideas. We prayed together, if it pleased Him, for a daughter with a tender heart toward Him. I also prayed

- She'd look like Steve: tall and with his wonderful blue eyes. I asked Him, if it pleased Him, to make her pretty, but not so pretty she would trust in her beauty. I was remembering Agur's prayer in Proverbs 30:8–9, where he asks God to give him neither poverty (for he might steal) nor riches (for he might profane the name of God).
- She'd have talents she could use for God's glory and be smart, but not so smart that she'd trust in her own wisdom.

Three months went by and there was no pregnancy. I was shocked and grieved, for I had been so sure it would happen. Yet His Spirit reminded me that He had led Steve and me to have the same plan, and now it was time for me to trust and obey. I went back on birth control.

In *The Papa Prayer,* Larry Crabb differentiates between a "me-centered" prayer life and a "relationally centered" prayer life.[7] In a me-centered prayer life, you are constantly asking God to make circumstances in your life favorable. But in a relationally centered prayer life, you are seeking *His* will, surrendering your will, and asking Him to change your heart if necessary to align with His. When I went back on birth control, that is what I was endeavoring to do, and I asked God to make me content with the wonderful sons we had.

Two months later, at summer's end, I was visiting with my friend Betsy on her family's dock overlooking Green Bay. She asked whether Steve and I planned to have any more children. I told her, "No. We feel this is the family God wants us to have." What I did not know was that little Sally had already begun growing in me, for God gave her to us *after* I went back on birth control.

Isn't that just like God? Birth control is not an obstacle for Him! He is such a God of surprises. And just as Sarah and Abraham believed Isaac was a miracle baby, because the odds were certainly against conception, we had that same sense.

That fall, I began leading an evangelistic Bible study for residents' wives, for Steve was in his residency to specialize in orthopedic surgery. A few had come to Christ, and

I was also endeavoring to teach them how to talk to God. They were too scared to pray out loud, but I had each write down a prayer request and give it to the woman on her right to pray over that week.

When I saw the requests, they were either for someone very distant (their uncle Ed's neighbor) or so general (that God would bless their family) that they wouldn't even know if God had answered their prayers. I encouraged them, "Please be personal and specific!" One of the women asked me to illustrate.

I decided to tell them the story of my pregnancy and of how specifically we had prayed for this child. They looked stunned. One said, "Do you really believe you can pray these things into happening?"

"You never know what God will do, but James says, 'You do not have, because you do not ask' [James 4:2]. He also tells us to pray according to God's will. We honestly didn't know what His will was in this case, so we asked for what we would like, but we also told Him that if He had a better idea, that's what we wanted." I told them I wouldn't want to miss being a mother to a Charles Spurgeon or a Dietrich Bonhoeffer!

Their eyes were full of wonder, and as the months passed, their faith and excitement grew until they were more convinced than I was that God would give us a daughter.

In the beginning of my ninth month, when I walked into the Bible study, they shouted, "Surprise!" They were throwing me a baby shower—for a girl! This was before routine ultrasounds, so we still did not know the gender, but they felt certain enough to have made us a pink baby quilt. Each had embroidered a square that had to do with little girls or the promises of God. I thought, *What have I done? Will the buds of their new and tender faith shrivel up if I give birth to a boy?*

Steve laughed when I brought home the quilt. "You got yourself into this one!" Then he said, "Since you've gone this far out on the limb, you might as well go all the way. They posted the surgery schedule for the week you are due, and I'll be in surgery every single day except April 27. So why don't you ask your friends to pray our baby will arrive on the 27th?"

I did. They prayed with real faith while I squirmed, hoping the limb I was out on would not break.

Sure enough, I went into labor in the wee hours of the morning of April 27. I still remember Steve's great cry: "God gave us a girl—and she looks just like me!"

The doctor and the nurses laughed, but indeed Sally is nearly a clone of her father: his long legs, his fair complexion, and his beautiful blue eyes. (I marvel now that God led me to pray she would look like him, for He knew I would cherish this reminder of Steve when He took Steve early. She not only looks like Steve, but she also has his wonderful joyful nature.) The women in my Bible study were beyond excited and began telling all their friends. Truly, it was a great celebration, and our God Hunt bulletin board was absolutely covered with cards rejoicing over answered prayer, exclaiming, "The LORD has done great things" (Psalm 126:3).

## Sow Your Tears

Returning to Psalm 126, remember that this psalm was written *not* in a time of joy but in a time of suffering and seeming silence from God. So after beginning his prayer by remembering a time when God astonished His people by reversing their fortune and filling their mouths with laugher, now the psalmist pleads for God to do it again:

> Restore our fortunes, O LORD,
>     like streams in the Negeb!
>     —verse 4

The Negeb River (the name means "dry" or "parched") could change overnight from a dry riverbed to a torrent when it rained, causing the underground streams to rise. The psalmist longs for God to come to him again, dramatically turning his dry soul into a river of joy.

So here is the question: How do we sow our tears so that God can reverse our barrenness?

It is clear that going out "weeping" is permissible—we are not to pretend and put on a happy face. But what is "the seed for sowing" that we are to plant *while* we are weeping? I believe it is the promises of God and the evidence in our lives and in history that God is good and trustworthy. We are repeatedly exhorted to "forget not all his benefits" (Psalm 103:2) and remind our souls of His promises:

> My eyes are awake before the watches of the night,
>     that I may meditate on your promise.
>     —Psalm 119:148

In fact, the psalmist of Psalm 126 closes not by thanking God for a reversal of fortune but by holding on to a promise:

> Those who sow in tears
>     shall reap with shouts of joy!
> He who goes out weeping,
>     bearing the seed for sowing,
> shall come home with shouts of joy,
>     bringing his sheaves with him.
> —verses 5–6

One day, even if what we so earnestly pleaded for was not granted in this life, our sorrow will indeed be turned to joy. For though God doesn't always reverse our hard circumstances, if we trust Him and don't back away, He strengthens our character and enlarges our hearts.

Jonathan Edwards wrote, "There are different degrees of happiness and glory in heaven."[8] Those who have trusted God in sorrow on this earth have been refined and will come forth as gold (Job 23:10). We will rejoice and not be jealous of hearts and rewards greater than our own, for there will be no sin in our hearts to mar our contentment.

So though God may or may not reverse our fortunes on earth, He definitely will reverse them in heaven. When one faith healer flew to our home during Steve's cancer, he told us, "God told me that if I came, Steve would be healed."

Steve asked, "Did He tell you if I would be healed on earth or in heaven?"

The man paused and then said, "No, He didn't."

I know God can heal on earth, and we truly believed He might heal Steve on earth. But it is also true, as you will see when we get to Isaiah, that some are taken early to be spared calamity. And when they trust Him despite His seeming silence, as Steve did, God sees and remembers. As J. B. Phillips paraphrases 2 Corinthians 4:17, "These little troubles (which are really so transitory) are winning for us a permanent, glorious and solid reward out of all proportion to our pain."

This is the promise of our God, who invites us to cry out to Him in our pain, knowing He will one day offer us a harvest of joy.

As a group, view the related video and share comments: go to deebrestin.com and click on *The Jesus Who Surprises* under Free Teaching Videos. Also, as an option for going deeper, listen online to "Praying Our Tears" by Tim Keller.

### Week Seven God Hunt

This week you will be practicing authenticity in your prayer life. When you lament, remember to listen, for lament can open up a dialogue with God. Be still and see if He gives you comfort or wisdom or reminds you of His character. Record these things in your "Today I spied God when . . ." notes.

### Day One: Chapter Review

1. Read the chapter and highlight as you read. Write down two thoughts that impressed you and share at least one with the group.

2. If you listened to "Praying Our Tears," what do you remember?

*Today I spied God when . . .*

### Day Two: Psalm 13, a Model of a Lament

The classic lament has three parts: (1) an honest expression of feelings, (2) a turn, where the psalmist remembers God's character, and (3) a resolve to trust God amid difficult circumstances.

3. Read Psalm 13 and see if you can identify the three parts of this lament with verse numbers:

   a.

   b.

   c.

4. Now try this with a lament of your own. Honestly express your feelings about a problem in your life, stop and listen, and then resolve to trust God. (You may or may not wish to share this with the group, but be authentic with God.)

   a.

   b.

   c.

*Today I spied God when . . .*

## *Day Three: The First Lamenter: Job*

God allowed Satan to sift Job, for God knew Job would come forth like gold and show sufferers in the future *how* to lament to stay close to God and receive wisdom. Prepare your heart for today's study by listening to Nicole Mullen sing "My Redeemer Lives" on YouTube.

5. Describe Job's lament in Job 14:1–6. How honest is he with God?

6. Find Job's question to God in verse 4. What does he think the answer is?

7. Read verses 7–14.

   a. Why does Job think a tree is better off than a man?

   b. What question does Job ask in verses 10 and 14?

   c. What wish is expressed in verse 13?

*8. During the time of the Old Testament, the afterworld was shadowy, and believers were not confident of heaven. Job does receive an answer, but it is a bit hard to see. Job's question, which you noted above, is "If a man dies, shall he live again?" Then, God's Spirit gives Job the answer, showing him to "wait" until his release from the grave, or "renewal," will come (verse 14). Find, in the passage below, what God's Spirit shows Job will happen on the day of his (and our) bodily resurrection.

> You will call and I will answer you;
>     you will long for the creature your hands have made.
> Surely then you will count my steps
>     but not keep track of my sin.
> My offenses will be sealed up in a bag;
>     you will cover over my sin.
>     —verses 15–17 (NIV)

9. Read the lament of 19:17–27.

   a. What are Job's honest feelings in verses 17–22?

   b. What turn, what wish, does Job express toward God in verses 23–24?

   c. In verses 25–27, Job articulates the amazing vision that God has burned in his heart. This vision is "engraved" (verse 24) in the words of Scripture, in Handel's *Messiah,* and in the hearts of believers forevermore. What is it?

*Today I spied God when . . .*

## Day Four: God Comes to Job from a Whirlwind

All through his suffering, Job has lamented, stayed close to God, and asked for answers. Finally, at the close, it comes.

10. Read Job 38:1–3. Describe how God comes and what He says initially to Job.

11. Read Job 38–41 and find two descriptions that put you in awe of God.

12. Read 42:1–6.

   a. What conclusion does Job reach in verse 3?

   b. Compare Job 42:1–6 to Psalm 131. What similarity do you see, and what do you learn from this about calming your anxious soul?

   c. What change has occurred in Job, according to Job 42:5–6?

13. In verses 7–9, what does God ask of Job's friends and why? How do they respond?

14. Job was relatively innocent and suffered almost unto death. His friends failed to comfort him, and indeed Job felt forsaken even by God. In what ways can you see Jesus as being "the greater Job"?

*Today I spied God when . . .*

## Day Five: Psalm 126, in Joy or in Sorrow

15. Read aloud Psalm 126. What do you notice most about this psalm?

16. Psalm 126 takes place in a time of great trouble, though we do not know what it is. But the psalmist begins his prayer time not with a lament or a supplication but with remembering a time of great faithfulness in the past. How does he describe it in verses 1–3? Why do you think he does this?

17. What does the psalmist ask of God in verse 4, and what metaphor does he use? (The Negev/Negeb is a dry desert area with a "wadi," a dry riverbed that wells up and flows with water when the torrential rains come.)

18. According to verses 5–6, what will happen to the person who "sow[s] in tears"?

19. Some Christians believe that we should stuff our tears in order to be good witnesses. Have you observed this? What do you think it means to grieve with hope, as 1 Thessalonians 4:13 tells us to do?

20. Remembering God's mercies from the past can help us grieve with hope. Share, briefly, a time of seeing God's mercy in a particular situation.

21. What is your takeaway from this week's lesson?

*Today I spied God when . . .*

## Prayer Time

Begin with speaking out praises to God for mercies in the past. Then offer requests. Finally, take turns lifting up a lament or a question to God, with a moment of silence between each person's prayer.

# EIGHT

# The Surprising Fruit of Suffering

## Fullness of Joy

It's not that your heart isn't going to break; it's how you
let the brokenness be made into abundance afterward.

—ANN VOSKAMP

It stormed the day we buried my husband. It seemed fitting, for no matter how some
may wax eloquent about death, Scripture tells us it is an enemy (1 Corinthians 15:26).
Even Jesus weeps at the tomb of Lazarus (John 11:34–35).

Rain fell fiercely in icy sheets as we huddled under the ineffective canopy that
flapped wildly in the wind. Thunder drowned out Pastor Miller's words of comfort. He
finally gave up trying to be heard, and the men from Casperson Funeral Home began
to lower the coffin that hung suspended by ropes above the freshly dug grave. As the
ropes began to creak, Sally cried, "No! Don't! Please, not yet, not yet!" The men stopped
and she ran out, knelt in the mud, and clutched the edge of the coffin, sobbing. Her
oldest brother, JR, joined her on his knees, his suit ruined, his arm around her. Minutes
passed and I was conscious of the shivering crowd watching this heartbreaking scene.
Finally, I went and knelt beside my children. "Your dad is not in there. You will see him
again. Let the men put it down."

Our youngest two daughters, Beth and Annie, stayed under the canopy, frozen in
their grief. *How would they make it without him?* It was Steve who first broke through
Beth's attachment disorder. And it was Steve's love that had melted Annie, who had

been like a little stone when we adopted her from an orphanage in Seoul when she was five. She had not been like other little girls, for she did not laugh or cry. But love did its transforming work and she had become a beautiful and compassionate teenager, joining Youth With A Mission right out of high school. But then Steve got sick, she came home, and it was as if the White Witch of Narnia had returned and cast her wicked spell, turning our daughter into stone again.

Could the sun possibly break through a storm so severe?

## A Prowling Lion

In our suffering, we have an enemy who sees an opportunity. Satan is a prowling lion (1 Peter 5:8). A hungry lion hides in the tall grass, watching for the wounded wildebeest that can't keep up with the herd. The lion spots it and bounds out with long strides, easily overtaking the helpless animal, ripping it to bloody pieces.

In the same way, Satan spies us when we're wounded and comes with his lies. Weakened, we are prone to believe him and back away from those who love us: other believers or God Himself. A sheep separated from the fold is an easy target.

One day just weeks after Steve's death, I heard Sally and Annie quarrelling downstairs, hurling insults at each other, accusing each other: "You weren't really there for Dad!"

I could almost smell that snake. He had slithered in with his lies. Sally and Annie *had* been there for Steve, not perfectly, but they both had made sacrifices. Sally was studying at the San Francisco Art Institute, a dream come true for her. But she dropped out and came home to be with her dad that whole year. Annie had sat by her dad's side as chemo dripped into him.

I sprinted down the stairs and gathered my girls in a hug, and we cried together. I coaxed them to lie down beside me, on Sally's bed, one on either side. I held them, stroked their hair, and waited for the storm to subside. When their sobs lessened, I told them, "Your sister is not your enemy. Your enemy is Satan. He wants to turn you against each other. He wants to turn you against God. That's how he wins. Let's make his plan backfire."

They were quiet, listening—I hoped.

"We all have regrets about last year. I do too. But we have a God who empathizes with our weaknesses. He forgives. He also longs for us to come to Him, to talk to Him, to tell Him what we are really feeling."

Annie said, "I can't."

"Just say 'Help.' If you can't say it out loud, say it in your heart."

She shook her head. "No."

Yet one sleepless night soon after that, Annie lay in her bed and said in her heart, *Help.*

Annie testifies that though the change was not immediate, God came to her slowly. He calmed her heaving soul, He brought loving Christians into her life, and one day He surprised her by shining an illuminating light into her darkness.

## Beauty for Ashes

Annie was the child Steve and I were not sure we should send to college. She had not been motivated to study in high school, and her grades had been poor. She said she saw no purpose in algebra, chemistry, or, for that matter, any of her classes. But she did have an interest in missions, so we directed her toward a year of missions. She joined Youth With A Mission, and a year turned into more: months in AIDS orphanages in Africa, in safe houses for girls in Thailand, and in drug-infested city ghettos. But when Steve died, she quit YWAM for good, defeated, disappointed in God, and again without purpose for her life.

After her silent cry of help, she decided to enroll in a few classes at our local university, just a block from our home. I am convinced now it was God's first response to her cry.

One class she chose was Ethics, a required philosophy class for premedical students. It was taught by Dr. David Rozema, who was an elder at our church. He assigned Aleksandr Solzhenitsyn's novel *Cancer Ward,* which skillfully portrays how caring, or the lack of it, on the part of medical professionals impacts patients.

One day Dr. Rozema asked the class members to raise their hands if they thought a nurse or a doctor who was skilled but also uncaring could still be a good nurse or doctor. Annie was amazed to see most of the hands go up. They had obviously missed the point of the novel, whereas all the way through, Annie kept thinking of her dad. Steve was an excellent spine surgeon, but the reason our small-town paper headlined "Beloved Doctor Dies" on the day after his death was due to Steve's great heart. He cared so deeply for his patients, praying fervently for each one, not charging the poor, and making house calls to both patients and their families.

At that moment, Annie decided she would study hard and become a nurse and carry on her father's legacy. She did exactly that, persevering through college and graduating from nursing school with flying colors. When she first started an internship at Good Samaritan Hospital, she told me, "What I am mostly doing right now is cleaning up after patients who have been sick. Mom, I think it is what I was born to do. They need someone who cares and doesn't make them feel ashamed and who can love them with the love of Christ. It gives me such joy, the kind of joy Dad had."

Annie went on to marry a godly young man, and they have three beautiful children, including a son named Steven. She is now studying to be a nurse practitioner—as a straight-A student. When I asked her if my writing about her poor performance in high school embarrassed her, she said, "No! It will give parents hope. What matters so often is the heart. God changed my heart, giving me a motivation to study." Today Annie's life is full of joy, not despite the sorrow but *because* of it.

## The Shaking of Our World

Satan can do nothing without God's permission, and God gives Satan only enough rope to hang himself. God knows the shaking of our world can awaken us to understand what is transitory and what is eternal. If we press into Him, we will discover what can never be shaken. And one day, we are told, He will shake all of creation:

> All of creation will be shaken and removed, so that only unshakable things will remain.
>
> Since we are receiving a Kingdom that is unshakable, let us be thankful and please God by worshiping him with holy fear and awe. For our God is a devouring fire.
>
> —Hebrews 12:27–29, NLT

Understanding what cannot be shaken is transformative, for we then more firmly set our affections on the things above. I once asked Dr. Darrell Bock of Dallas Seminary which sections of the Old Testament he thought Jesus showed the two on the walk to

Emmaus. He thought the Old Testament passages that Peter and Paul quote in their first sermons give us a clue. In Acts, both Peter and Paul turn to Psalm 16, so we will turn there too and learn the surprising secret of how sorrow for the believer can actually *produce* joy.

## The Sorrows of Those Who Run After Another God

In the days of the psalmist, people would turn for help to gods of rain, fertility, war, or healing because they didn't think the one true God could help them. In the same way today, if we think God cannot meet our needs, we run after prosperity, position, or people instead of running to Him.

As believers, we can be blind to what we are doing, for we are still involved in religious activities—"doing God" but *running* after what we think will make us happy. And yet as Psalm 16:4 tells us, "The sorrows of those who run after another god will multiply." This echoes the language of the curse in Genesis 3:16, when God told Eve, "I will surely multiply your pain in childbearing."

In recent years, God multiplied my pain when I was using manipulation to try to control my administrative assistants and my adult children, but that pain, along with excellent Bible teaching on heart idols, brought me to my senses and compelled me to turn and run instead to God. He showed me a more excellent way: to either speak the truth in love or be silent, pray, and trust Him to work with my assistants and adult children. And the restoration of those relationships and the sense of His presence, indeed, gave me joy. I have experienced the fulfillment of the promises of Psalm 16:

> You make known to me the path of life;
> in your presence there is fullness of joy;
> at your right hand are pleasures forevermore.
> —verse 11

When God shakes our world, if we come to our senses and run instead to Him, what we discover is that "in [His] presence there is fullness of joy." I see this in the prisons all the time. The women in the ministry in which I'm privileged to work[1] have opted to move into a section of the prison designated as a faith dorm. There they are discipled by volunteers four nights a week, diligently studying the Scriptures and learning to put their trust fully in God. Though God has shaken their world and they have lost so much, they are experiencing His presence and an amazing fullness of joy. Every time I go to these women, I leave thinking, *It is true, Lord. They have nothing, and yet they have everything that really matters. They have You. And in Your presence is fullness of joy.*

## Jesus Hidden in Psalm 16

But something else is in Psalm 16, and it is the portion Peter quotes in his first sermon:

> I have set the LORD always before me;
>> because he is at my right hand, I shall not be shaken.
> —verse 8

David didn't *always* set the Lord before him. He sexually abused Bathsheba, using his power as king to take advantage of her. When she became pregnant, David had her husband, Uriah, his loyal friend, put at the front of the line in the battle so that he would die. And God *did* shake David's world to awaken him. He sent Nathan the prophet to expose his sin and bring David to repentance. So we see that David is actually referring to Jesus here—someone who was *never* shaken.

The psalm goes on to say:

> Therefore my heart is glad, and my whole being rejoices;
>> my flesh also dwells secure.
> For you will not abandon my soul to Sheol,
>> or let your holy one see corruption.
> —verses 9–10

David's body *did* see corruption, but there is One whose body did not. We know this portion of the psalm also refers to Jesus, for when Peter quotes this passage, he refers to Jesus, whom they crucified but who has been raised up and is Lord and Christ (Acts 2:29–32). And how do the listeners respond? They are "cut to the heart" and three thousand souls are added to the early church (verses 37–41).

You may be "cut to the heart" when you first turn to Christ, or you may be "cut to the heart" when He reveals idols of the heart in your life. That is a good thing, for like a skillful surgeon removes shrapnel from a wounded soldier, our God removes the shrapnel from our stony hearts and replaces it with flesh. It may hurt, but oh, the healing that will come!

## The Lord Is My Chosen Portion and My Cup

When David's world is shaken, he sees and holds to the truth that can sustain us as well. In Psalm 16 he also says,

> The LORD is my chosen portion and my cup;
> you hold my lot.
> The lines have fallen for me in pleasant places;
> indeed, I have a beautiful inheritance.
> —verses 5–6

The word *cup* often refers to suffering, as when Jesus prays in Gethsemane, "My Father, if it be possible, let this cup pass from me" (Matthew 26:39). When we realize that the Lord is in control, a peace comes to us, despite the suffering. We realize that this shaking is temporary and that we have an inheritance that can never be taken from us.

When the Lord gave portions of land to the people of Israel, the priests were given no land, for the Lord told them, "I am your portion and your inheritance" (Numbers 18:20). Is it possible to have everything taken from you and still have joy? Yes! I see it in prison. And Charles Spurgeon writes, "Martyrs have been happy in dungeons."[2] From where does this joy come? It comes from the Lord Himself, who fills us.

Again, this is where Christianity differs from the other religions—other religions give you teachings but no life-giving power. But as Paul tells the Athenians, who were worshipping an "unknown god" (Acts 17:23), there *is* a revealed God, who rose from the dead, and in Him, "we live and move and have our being" (verse 28). Our God lives, sees, and comes to us with comfort and even joy, a joy that indeed surprises us, like the sun breaking through the fiercest storm.

### Bible Study Eight

As a group, view the related video and share comments: go to deebrestin.com and click on *The Jesus Who Surprises* under Free Teaching Videos. Also, as an option for going deeper, listen online to "Removing Idols of the Heart" by Tim Keller.

## Week Eight God Hunt

When God's Spirit convicts you about something, that is a divine encounter. Be aware of times when this happens, and notice how you respond. Also continue to record under the "Today I spied God when . . ." sections any daily gifts, verses that resonate with you, and answers to prayer.

## Day One: Chapter Review

1.  After reading and highlighting the chapter, write down two thoughts that impressed you to share with the group.

2.  If you listened to "Removing Idols of the Heart," what did you learn?

*Today I spied God when . . .*

## Day Two: The Stonecutter

Psalm 16 deals with idols of the heart, those "stones" that keep us from experiencing God. We're going to begin, therefore, by looking at Ezekiel and a metaphor God uses to show us how to respond so that we might experience growth and fullness of joy. Spiritual growth requires two steps: something must be recognized and removed, and something must, by faith, replace what has been removed.

3. Read Ezekiel 36:25–27.

   a. What makes us unclean, or to put it another way, what is the sin beneath our sin, according to verse 25?

   b. The sprinkling of clean water is a metaphor for the cleansing of God when we repent of our idols. To recognize and repent from an idol, ask yourself, *In what area do I tend to yield to temptation? What need am I trying to fulfill for myself that God could fill? What false identity am I clinging to other than being a beloved child of God?*

   *c. Jesus alludes to this passage from Ezekiel in John 3:5. What insight does this give you into what He tells Nicodemus?

   d. The second part of the process of growth is described in Ezekiel 36:26–27. Idols cannot be removed but only replaced. With what do we need to allow God to replace them, according to this passage?

4. Let's look at how to apply Ezekiel 36:25–27 to our lives. For instance, the next time you are lying awake during the night, worrying about something, how could you use the gospel and remembrance of God's faithfulness in the past to speak the truth to your soul? Be specific regarding the words you would use.

5. Many of us have a habit of getting angry when things don't go our way. We might honk unnecessarily at someone on the road or even throw something. This might be because of a control idol or because we believe a false identity about ourselves, such as we need to be perfect to be loved. How might we repent and speak to our souls in those cases?

*Today I spied God when . . .*

## Day Three: The Sorrows of Those Who Run After Another God

We love our heart idols and we don't want to let them go, so the psalmist helps us see the truth so that we might be strengthened to truly repent and trust.

6. Read Psalm 16:1–5.

   a. Of what does David remind himself in verses 2–3? How does this inspire confidence in God?

b. According to verse 4, what happens to those who run after another god?

c. Share a personal example of your running after "another god," or rebelling against God's way, and experiencing multiplied "sorrows." It doesn't have to be choosing something bad. We create idols out of good things, such as friendship and ministry, when we find our identity or security in them.

d. What happens, according to verses 5–6, to the person who makes the Lord his chosen portion and cup?

e. The tribe of Levi, or the priests of Israel, were given no land like the others to remind them that the Lord was their inheritance. How could this help you as you ponder financial losses or decisions?

*Today I spied God when . . .*

## Day Four: How Sorrow Can Produce Joy in a Believer's Heart

7. Read Psalm 16:7–11.

a. What does God give David (verse 7)?

b. Hebrews tells us that God is going to shake our world. But what will happen if we set the Lord always before us, according to Psalm 16:8?

c. Sometimes the shaking of our world causes us to realize the futility of our idols. The only One who will never let us down, move away, or die is the Lord. Describe a time you experienced a shaking of your world that helped you to press into God and experience joy.

d. How do you see joy in the psalmist in verse 9?

e. How does verse 10 show you we are no longer talking about David?

f. What three joys await us if we make the Lord our refuge, according to verse 11?

*Today I spied God when . . .*

## Day Five: Cut to the Heart

Peter and Paul both turn to Psalm 16 to explain the gospel in their first sermons. They show us how Jesus is hidden in the psalm, and the response of their listeners illustrates what is necessary for spiritual growth.

8. Read Acts 2:22–36.

  a. What does Peter tell the crowd in verses 22–24?

  b. In verses 25–28, Peter quotes Psalm 16. To whom does he say it refers and why?

9. Read Acts 2:37–41.

  a. Remembering Ezekiel, what first step of growth do you observe in the listeners?

  b. How do you see the second step of growth promised and received?

10. Jesus tells Nicodemus, "Unless one is born of water and the Spirit, he cannot enter the kingdom of God" (John 3:5). Jesus is alluding to Ezekiel, offering a picture of what happens to one who repents and trusts Christ. Have you been born again? If so, share in a sentence on what basis you believe you are in the kingdom of God.

11. What is your takeaway from this week and why?

*Today I spied God when . . .*

## Prayer Time

Take turns speaking a heart idol out loud, with others supporting each individual with sentence prayers.

# NINE

# Our Secret Weapon

## Learning from the Psalms How to Pray

> Have you realized that most of your unhappiness in life is
> due to the fact that you are listening to yourself instead of
> talking to yourself?
>
> —D. MARTYN LLOYD-JONES

God knew the storm of Steve's cancer was coming, so I believe He led Steve and me, individually, years before, to develop the habit of praying the psalms. When Steve first told me that his New Year's resolution for 2000 was to read through all three massive volumes of Charles Spurgeon's commentaries on the Psalms, I doubted that even he could accomplish that. Yet, at the end of the year, as we sat together reading by the lights of the Christmas tree, Steve gently closed volume 3 and whispered, "I've spent this year in the presence of a very godly man."

At the same time Steve was reading Spurgeon, I was reading a much smaller book by Dietrich Bonhoeffer, titled *Psalms: The Prayer Book of the Bible*. This comment in particular had a profound impact on me:

> It is a dangerous error, certainly very widespread among Christians, to think that
> the heart can pray by itself. . . . Prayer does not mean simply to pour out one's
> heart. It means rather to find the way to God and to speak with him, whether
> the heart is full or empty. . . . If we wish to pray with confidence and gladness,
> then the words of Holy Scripture will have to be the solid basis of our prayer.[1]

Bonhoeffer didn't mean we shouldn't pour out our hearts to God, for Psalm 62:8 tells us to do just that, but he *was* saying that when we use God's prayer book to guide us, our prayers will widen not only in scope but also in fruitfulness, for we will be praying within God's will.

Steve encouraged me to write a Bible study on the Psalms and to work with Integrity Music to put a CD in that guide with those psalms set to music. (This would later become the Bible study *A Woman of Worship*.) It was such a sweet year as we listened together to hundreds of psalm songs, choosing our favorites. We discovered there are many psalms that, rather than speaking to God, show the psalmist taking his soul in hand and speaking to her. (The soul is feminine in Scripture.) One of Steve's favorite passages like that was this one:

Remember your word to your servant,
    in which you have made me hope.
This is my comfort in my affliction,
    that your promise gives me life.
—119:49–50

Steve explained that the psalmist wasn't asking God to remember, for God doesn't forget, but he was asking God to help *him* remember His Word so that he could speak those words of life to his anxious soul. Steve wished we had a psalm-song for this passage, but Integrity hadn't sent us one.

Suddenly he said, "I feel sure they have one—they just didn't send it."

"I think they sent everything they had," I said, not wanting to be a pest to the people at Integrity.

But Steve's comment nettled me, and finally I picked up the phone and called Integrity. "Might you possibly have a song based on Psalm 119:49–50, the one that says 'I hope in Your Word'?"

"We do!" the woman at Integrity said. "And that's what it is called. Didn't we send it? It's so beautiful! I'll get it right to you!"

Steve and I melted when we heard it. We thought it the most beautiful song on the whole CD. It is also one of those benefits I do not want to forget, for I feel God gave it to us to prepare us for the hurricane headed our way.

## Our Song in the Night

D. Martyn Lloyd-Jones, who was both a medical doctor and a pastor, emphasized that to find your way out of spiritual depression and anxiety, you must stop *listening* to your soul and start *speaking* to her the very truths of God. Our souls are not quiet ponds but swirling whirlpools.

After Steve's diagnosis, when I looked ahead to a possible future without him and *listened to my soul,* this is what I heard:

- You'll never make it without Steve.
- Your daughters won't make it. He is the one who
  brought light to Annie's and Beth's darkness!
  Already, they are regressing back into that
  darkness.
- If Steve dies, your joy will be over.

But if I spoke to my soul the truths of the Psalms, I could calm those swirling waters. I would remind my soul:

- God is a father to the fatherless (68:5).
- God is a protector of widows (68:5).
- In God's presence there is fullness of joy (16:11).

Before Steve's diagnosis, the two of us often laughed that we had become "codependent insomniacs." If one of us couldn't sleep, the sleepless one would whisper to the sleeping one, "Are you awake?" And then we'd *both* be awake! Growing up, our children told us they loved hearing us talking and laughing in bed, sensing the security that comes when parents love one another.

After Steve's diagnosis, I tried *not* to wake him, for he so needed sleep. But often I couldn't stop crying, and that awakened him. He suggested that we both memorize Psalm 103 to help us calm our souls in the night. Throughout this whole psalm, David is speaking not to God but to his soul. So we did likewise, praying through Psalm 103 often in the night, and God calmed our anxious souls.

The prayers Psalm 103 inspired would yield amazing fruit in the decade to come. They helped us, as we saw in Psalm 126, "sow in tears." It is a story that I'm excited to tell you later in this chapter. But first I want you to see how this psalm can give you power for effectual soul talk.

## Forget Not All His Benefits

David begins this prayer by telling his soul, repeatedly, to bless the Lord and remember all His benefits:

> Bless the LORD, O my soul,
>> and all that is within me,
>> bless his holy name!
>
> Bless the LORD, O my soul,
>> and forget not all his benefits.
>
> —Psalm 103:1–2

Here David seems to be exhorting us to review our God Hunts so we don't forget. This is especially important in times when God seems silent.

Steve and I took turns remembering the times when God surprised us. He reminded me of the first time Annie saw God answer a prayer. She was in second grade. She'd been out of the orphanage only two years and was fearful of authority figures, since the ones she had known had been severe.

Annie's second-grade teacher had been quite stern with her about a lost library book, and Annie had searched for it diligently without success. She pleaded to stay home from school the next day, but I sent her off, thinking she'd get grace. When I picked her up, she burst into tears, telling of another scolding. I wanted to march in and tell that woman to show this little girl mercy, for heaven's sake, but I decided to cool it for one more day. I told Annie that if we didn't find *Mr. Popper's Penguins* before school the next morning, I'd walk into class with her, talk to the teacher, and pay for the book.

That night, after another fruitless search, I tucked a very sad and scared little girl into bed. I prayed over her again not only that God might show us where that book was but also that she would be able to fall asleep and have a good dream.

That night, Annie had a great dream! In the dream, she saw that the book had fallen behind her other books in her closet and was wedged behind the middle of the third shelf. She woke, walked right to that third shelf, parted the books in the middle, and there it was, the penguins smiling out at her. Steve remembered how she came running down the stairs, waving the softcover book in the air, and crying, "Jesus did it! Jesus did it!"

Years later, together in the nights both literal and figurative, Steve and I helped one another recount God's mercies to us, stirring our souls to trust in this time of trouble.

As we memorized—which is such a great help in meditation—we also discussed passages that puzzled us. One such passage in Psalm 103 was this:

> Bless the LORD, O my soul,
>     and forget not all his benefits,
> who forgives all your iniquity,
>     who heals all your diseases.
>     —verses 2–3

"But He doesn't heal all our diseases," I said.

Steve answered, "Yes, He does. If not on earth, in heaven. For believers. And this also may be talking about soul sickness, for David is talking to his soul."

I was quiet. I so wanted my husband healed on earth—in body, not "just" soul!

And yet, now that Steve has gone to be with the Lord, there is so much comfort in knowing that he is not just alive but healthy again, healed of that terrible cancer that ravaged his beautiful body. I will see him again, and he will have a resurrected body that is strong and will never grow old or be sick! We will hug and talk and never have to part again.

## His Days Are Like Grass

Psalm 103 also reminds us of the contrast between the frailty of earthly man and the steadfast love of the Lord. This is the passage that led Steve and me to our most painful and yet most fruitful prayers:

> As for man, his days are like grass;
>     he flourishes like a flower of the field;
> for the wind passes over it, and it is gone.
>     —verses 15–16

After Steve first recited those words in the dark, we were silent, both sensing that God might be calling Steve home despite our earnest prayers for healing. Though we had been pleading for Steve's healing on earth, I think this was the moment we realized it might not happen. I say this because it is important to acknowledge that prayer is not getting God to give you what *you* want but dialoguing with Him, listening to Him, submitting to Him, and asking Him to give you what *He* wants, even if it is costly.

I have beloved friends and relatives who would say it is never God's will for cancer to win. They exhorted us to pray with faith and not receive that thought. But is this true scripturally?

First, we know "it is appointed for man to die" (Hebrews 9:27). Every single one of us will die of something—that is what God appointed. But is it ever God's will for the righteous to die young? Isaiah tells us, "Yes."

> The righteous man perishes,
> and no one lays it to heart;
> devout men are taken away,
> while no one understands.
> For the righteous man is taken away from calamity;
> he enters into peace.
> —57:1–2

While from our earthly point of view we look at death as perishing, from God's point of view, death for the righteous means life, health, peace, and a great welcome by so many on the other side. I have a photograph of a sailboat disappearing over the horizon to remind me that though Steve seems to have also disappeared, he is actually just out of sight. He was welcomed, on the other shore, with shouts of, "Here he comes!"

We rarely know, on this side of eternity, why people die young, so it can be painful when others try to give us reasons. It made Elisabeth Elliot angry when people told her that her husband Jim was speared by the Auca Indians so that she could forgive them and bring them to faith. She wrote, "God is God. If He is God, He is worthy of my worship and my service. I will find rest nowhere but in His will, and that will is infinitely, immeasurably, unspeakably beyond my largest notions of what He is up to."[2]

God's ways, Isaiah tells us, are not our ways. That night, as Steve and I dialogued with God through Psalm 103, we sensed that He might be taking us in the opposite direction from where we wanted to go, just as Jesus tells Peter that one day someone will "lead you where you do not want to go" (John 21:18, NIV).

Steve didn't want to die because he didn't want to leave us, but he knew that for him death would lead to peace and unimaginable joy. So our next question to the Lord was, *If this is Your plan, what about the people Steve leaves behind? Me? Our five children?* Our sons were out of the nest, but our daughters were not.

In the very next stanza of Psalm 103 after "His days are like grass," God answered,

The steadfast love of the LORD is from everlasting to everlasting
    on those who fear him,
  and his righteousness to children's children,
to those who keep his covenant
  and remember to do his commandments.
—verses 17–18

There was our answer. God would take care of us.

On the basis of that covenant promise, Steve was stirred to pray that we would love and trust God, if God was taking him home. He prayed that God would be a Father to the fatherless and a Husband to the widow. He prayed that if our three daughters did marry, they would marry godly men. He also prayed that God would send godly men to be fathers to the fatherless. He prayed for his future grandchildren, that they would trust and obey God. As painful as all this was for me to hear, Steve was sowing his tears, tears that have reaped a harvest above and beyond what we could have even imagined.

We never stopped praying for earthly healing. And yet I was able to release Steve when his suffering became intense, remembering this dialogue with God in the night. Shortly after that, on October 16, 2004, Steve entered into peace.

We grieved, but not as those without hope. In the midst of my own long journey through the river of grief, I was thankful that I had learned to speak to my soul. Indeed, those promises I was speaking to my soul started to be fulfilled. God began to surprise my children and me with answers to our psalm-prayers one after another, almost like dominoes neatly falling. God provided fathers for the fatherless for all three of our daughters.

## Reaping a Harvest from Tears

After Steve died, our son John and his wife, Julie, stepped up to care for Beth, our adopted daughter from Thailand who wanted to be on her own but wasn't ready to be entirely on her own. They offered her a room in their basement while she went to school in Kansas City. She would have both independence and protection.

Next was Sally, who was headed to Chicago for school that following summer. When I was speaking in Chicago that spring, Sally came with me and we had dinner with a former pastor and his wife, Greg and Ruth Scharf. Greg was head preaching professor at Trinity Seminary, and the moment he heard Sally planned to take classes at Trinity that summer, he invited her to live with them. Tears welled up in me, for it was such a clear answer to Steve's prayer. I couldn't have handpicked a better father to the fatherless for Sally or a better family for her to be placed in.

Steve's prayers for godly husbands for our daughters also bore fruit. A few months before Steve died, Sally's brother John wanted Sally to meet his good friend Phil. John sensed that they both would resist matchmaking. Knowing they both spoke Spanish, John came up with a clever ruse. He invited a few people who spoke Spanish over after church "to practice their rusty Spanish." He didn't mention to Sally that one of those people was their pastor's son, an eligible bachelor named Phil.

The ruse worked. Phil was smitten with Sally and she with him. Phil began making trips to see her in the last six months of Steve's life. I remember the August night when it became clear that Steve approved of Phil and felt he was God's answer to his prayers. We were seated on the back porch, lingering after dinner, watching the Nebraska sun sink beneath the trees and listening to the hum of cicadas. It was just two months before Steve's death, and he was weary. Yet suddenly he found the strength to stand. He placed a hand on Phil's head and another on Sally's head and prayed simply, "God, please bless this relationship."

We were all quiet.

Sally blushed, thinking, *Dad, what if Phil isn't that serious about me?*

Phil was quietly euphoric, for he *was* that serious about Sally and knew her father's blessing would hold great weight with her and with me.

A year and two weeks after Steve's death, in 2005, Phil and Sally married. Phil's dad presided at the wedding and asked, "Who gives this woman to this man?"

I could honestly say, "Her father and I do."

When Steve died, Annie quit YWAM and came back home. Our pastor, Mike Lano, told his son David he liked what he had seen in Annie Brestin and thought David might want to get to know her. I was speaking at a retreat, when Sally called me and said, "Something's going on with David Lano and Annie. He came over after church to help her paint her room, even though he was wearing very nice clothes. They've been down there all afternoon, laughing and talking."

Indeed, when I got home the next day, Annie told me that David was coming over that afternoon to ask if he could date her. I prayed, asking God for wisdom, asking for insight into what Steve would have said. I thought about how David owned a motorcycle and guns and how Steve never wanted his daughters near either one. He had explained, "The most difficult surgeries I do are on victims of motorcycle accidents or gunshots. It's like trying to put Humpty Dumpty together again. If they live, they are seldom ever the same."

So when David asked to date Annie, I told him that I liked him and that Steve would have too—but there was the motorcycle and gun problem. He knocked the air out of me when he responded immediately: "I'll sell them tomorrow."

When I got my breath back, I smiled. "Well, then, you may date Annie."

One night Annie and David had an argument, and Annie went to David's father for wisdom. Annie said, "Pastor Lano pulled his chair up close to me and looked at me intently. He was right there. He asked me to tell him everything and he *really* listened." God had provided a father for the fatherless for Annie as well.

David and Annie married two years later, in 2007. At their wedding, Annie's sister Beth invited a young man named Seth, another pastor's son, as her guest. It was my first time meeting Seth. Afterward he wrote me a thank-you note with this PS: "I own neither guns nor a motorcycle."

The writing was on the wall.

When Beth told me that Seth's father was a pastor to Asian international students and that his mother taught deaf students, I marveled. How equipped they would be to love Beth, our Asian daughter whose heavy accent was sometimes difficult to understand.

Still, I was concerned because neither Beth nor Seth had dated much and they had met through a Christian online dating site. When Beth first told me that she had met someone online and that I shouldn't be worried because he loved Jesus, I thought cynically, *He has seen your picture* [Beth is stunning] *and now he says he loves Jesus.* But Beth was convinced he really did love Jesus, and she and Seth decided, after three months of communicating, that it was time to meet face to face. Beth asked me, "Should I tell him that I am missing an arm now, or just let him find out when he meets me?"

I said, "Definitely tell him now. He may decide not to meet you, but this will be a good test of his character."

Beth's missing arm did not cause Seth to back off. Instead, he reasoned that the disability had helped to shape the strength of character that he was discovering through their online communication. That in itself told me a great deal about Seth and what he valued. A little over a year later, in 2008, Seth and Beth married. Seth's family warmly welcomed Beth and has loved her so well.

Within four years of Steve's death, our three daughters all married godly men who were sons of godly pastors. Coincidence? I don't think so. I attributed this to Steve's earnest psalm-prayers in the night that God be a Father to the fatherless.

But God certainly wasn't done surprising us.

## New Life

Sally and Phil didn't want to wait to have children, but wait they did. The wait was hard because Sally chose to go off her antidepressant, fearing it might affect a baby adversely. She plummeted back into the depths of depression, becoming incapacitated: fearful of being alone, struggling to eat and sleep, and weeping inconsolably. Her doctor advised her to go back on the antidepressant, assuring her the risk for the baby from Sally's particular prescription was infinitesimal.

Despite the hesitancy of some Christians to use antidepressants, I am so thankful for them, for both Steve and Sally had chemical imbalances that were remedied only when they finally went on antidepressants. Taking medication is a serious step, and before jumping into it, it is wise to get counseling, repent of any known sin, and practice healthy eating, sleeping, and exercise habits. But if there is a genuine chemical imbalance, antidepressants can be as great a gift as insulin is to diabetes, and penicillin to pneumonia.

We've also learned, the hard way, that after you go off an antidepressant, it may not be effective when you return to it. It took more than two years for the doctors to find another antidepressant for Sally that was effective, but finally our joyful Sally was back. There was still no pregnancy, but we had not given up hope. Many were praying fervently for her and Phil, and her brother JR told me he had a word from the Lord she would conceive. I so wanted to believe it!

On the fifth anniversary of Steve's death, I was in Chicago, where Sally and Phil lived, recording programs with Moody Radio about my book *The God of All Comfort*. Sally said she'd stop by my hotel room before work with breakfast so we could share happy memories about Steve. This anniversary is always hard, filled with difficult memories, so it was a gift to be together.

When Sally knocked, I expected to open the door and see a sad face, but instead she was grinning. I cocked my head, wondering what was up. She rushed in, put down the Starbucks lattes, whirled around, and exclaimed, "Mom, this isn't a sad day—this is a *great* day! Dad is rejoicing too. My pregnancy test this morning was POSITIVE!"

I was almost afraid to believe it, but indeed it was true. Sally was expecting a baby that June!

A few weeks after Sally's news, Annie called me, breathless from the shock, to tell me they were expecting. Their baby was due in early July.

Annie was in nursing school, so she and David had decided to wait for children, but that was not God's plan. I told Annie what Luci Shaw had told me once: "We have five children: we planned two and God planned three." We laughed, knowing God planned them all.

Beth and Seth were also planning to wait, but a few weeks after Annie's news, Beth called: "Mom, I'm pregnant! Our baby is due in early August!"

At this time my only son who was married was John, and he and Julie already had five children. They *did* hope to have one more, and indeed John called a few weeks after Beth's news to tell me, "Praise God—we're pregnant! The baby is due the middle of August!"

We were now expecting four babies in the summer of 2010.

## It's a Girl!

All three of my daughters and their husbands decided to find out the gender ahead of time, and one after another, they called to tell me: *"It's a girl!"*

John and Julie like to be surprised, so they didn't find out ahead of time, but indeed the fourth baby of the summer was a girl as well. They named her Octavia, for they had lost two children—with the two in heaven, she was their eighth.

So, in the summer of 2010, all of my daughters and my then only daughter-in-law gave birth to little girls. I was flying from one birth to another, and "our mouth was filled with laughter" (Psalm 126:2).

When I was together with my four daughters and their four daughters in public, questions would come.

"Oh my—are they quadruplets?"

"No—four single births to four daughters."

"Wow! Are they girls or boys?"

"All girls."

"That's incredible. Did you plan this?"

We laughed! *As if we could!* "No, God did this."

Indeed, we know He did. He is the Jesus who surprises, and may we never forget how He filled our mouths with laughter, how He turned our mourning into dancing, how He heard Steve's prayers in the night and bent down and answered.

But even more amazing than the gift of godly husbands, godly fathers-in-law, and quivers full of children is the growth we have experienced. Just as the bush that is severely pruned bears better fruit, so it is with us. My children are kinder and wiser because of the suffering they have been through, and I have experienced an intimacy with God I had not known was possible. The best books I have written have been in these years after Steve's death, for I have pressed into God like never before. But if you were to tell me that these were the reasons Steve had to die, I would give you a karate kick. I don't know why he died, but I can trust the One who does all things well in His time.

I also don't want the message of this chapter to be that the answer to life's heartaches is marriage and motherhood, for that is *not* what I am proclaiming. The answer to life's heartaches is surrendering to God and experiencing His sweet presence, trusting that He knows best what to give to or withhold from us. To illustrate this, I am so eager to tell you Sophia's story in our final chapter on the Psalms.

## Bible Study Nine

As a group, view the related video and share comments: go to deebrestin.com and click on *The Jesus Who Surprises* under Free Teaching Videos. Also, as an option for going deeper, listen online to the Fuller Studio recording of Eugene Peterson and Bono discussing the Psalms.

## Week Nine God Hunt

Learning to dialogue with God using the psalms and then being still before Him can help you hear from Him—He gives songs in the night, wisdom, and peace. Develop this habit and share below any ways you spy God as you pray Scripture or speak to your soul.

## Day One: Chapter Review

1. Read the chapter and highlight as you read. Write down two thoughts that impressed you and share one with the group.

2. If you listened to Eugene Peterson and Bono, what stood out to you?

*Today I spied God when . . .*

## Day Two: Speaking to Your Soul

3. Read Psalm 119:49–50. In this passage, what is the psalmist asking God to do and why?

4. If you listen to your soul in an area about something that concerns you, what might your soul say that would *increase* your anxiety? What are some promises from God's Word that you could speak to your soul to calm her?

5. Read Psalm 42 through and find the repeated refrain.

   a. What question is the psalmist asking of his soul, and what exhortation is he giving to his soul?

   b. The psalmist begins by using two water images to describe his despair. The first is in verse 1, of a deer *panting* for water but (on the basis of verse 2) not finding it. Using your sanctified imagination, describe a possible scenario for this deer and what the deer might be experiencing. Then share what insight this gives you into what the psalmist might be feeling.

   c. What is the only water the psalmist is experiencing, according to verse 3?

   d. Common symptoms of depression are not sleeping, not eating, continual crying, and feeling isolated. Find references to all of these in verses 3–4.

   e. In verses 5–6, though the psalmist seems to be isolated on a mountain, he remembers better days and speaks about them to his soul. What does he tell his soul? Is speaking to your soul a new concept for you?

*f. The psalmist now moves to two more water images that are simultaneously negative and positive. Describe these two water images found in verse 7.

*g. Compare this to Jonah 2:3. What insight does this give you into what the psalmist is feeling?

h. Read Psalm 42:8 and find what consoles the psalmist. Who is behind these waves, and how does that sustain the psalmist in the midst of terror?

i. How is verse 8 a comfort in your times of distress?

j. How can you see Jesus in verses 9–10? How might this comfort you in your trials?

k. In verse 11, the psalmist's soul spasms again, so what does he keep doing? (See also Psalm 43:5.)

*Today I spied God when . . .*

## Day Three: Forget Not All His Benefits

Psalm 103 is also a psalm in which the psalmist is speaking to his soul. Read verses 1–14.

6. What does the psalmist tell his soul in verses 1–2? What benefit or blessing do you remember from your life yesterday?

7. Read verses 3–5 and list some of the benefits he is remembering.

8. What pictures does the psalmist paint in verses 13–14 that show God's gentleness toward us? How does this give you comfort today?

*Today I spied God when . . .*

## Day Four: We Are Like Grass, but His Love Is Forever

9. What tender mercy can you share from yesterday?

10. Read Psalm 103:15–17 and describe the contrast you see.

11. This is the psalm that Dee and Steve prayed in the night and that shaped their dialogue with God. What stood out to you in their story?

12. According to Isaiah 57:1, is it ever God's plan for the righteous to die young? If so, why?

13. How did Psalm 103:17–18 cause Steve to pray? How was he sowing his tears? How are those tears reaping a harvest?

14. When you realize the frailty of this earthly life and the vast domain of eternity, how might that help you speak to your soul about transitory troubles? Give an example.

*Today I spied God when . . .*

### Day Five: Jesus Bled Scripture

Not only does Psalm 22 prophesy the atrocities Jesus would bear at the cross, but Jesus Himself quotes it at His moment of deepest agony. The suffering we see in this psalm, and which Jesus fulfills, should help us to speak clearly to our souls when the Enemy is telling us God does not love us.

15. Read verses 1–2. How does David begin his lament?

16. How can you see Jesus in verse 1? (See also Matthew 27:46.)

17. Why does God the Father turn His face away from His Son? (See Habakkuk 1:13.)

18. How can you see Jesus in Psalm 22:6–8?

19. How can you see Him in verses 12–15? How do we know this is only Christ now and not David?

20. How can you see Jesus in verses 16–18?

*Today I spied God when . . .*

## Prayer Time

Begin your prayer time with thanksgiving, using your God Hunt discoveries or Psalm 22:19–31 to help you. Then each person takes a turn voicing a fear or particular anxiety, with others speaking the promises of God or prayers of petition. For example:

**Tom:** I am anxious about my finances.
**Mark:** Lord, please give Tom peace that You are his Provider.
**Susan:** Yes, Lord.
**Sandy:** I am anxious about so many things, I can't even name them!
**Tom:** Father, may Sandy stay her mind on You and find the rest You promise.
**Susan:** Yes, Lord, please give her Your perfect peace.

# TEN

# A Royal Wedding Song

## When You Give Your Heart, You Need Not Fear

> To find him I had to let go of me. Or rather, let go of the
> me I had designed so carefully over the years.
>
> —SARA HAGERTY

Sophia is my new friend, a youthful Mary to my aging Elizabeth. She comes to my door fresh and dewy eyed, brimming with excitement, magnifying the Lord, for He has been mindful of her!

"I didn't know this kind of joy was possible," she exudes. "I used to find that five minutes in prayer felt like forever. But now, Dee! I cannot wait to be with Him, for He is calling me to come away with Him and I can be with Him for hours, for He surrounds me with His presence. I don't want this sweet season to stop!"

How did this twentysomething woman come upon the secret that eludes many believers for decades, if not their whole lives?

Through suffering.

A few years ago, fresh out of college, Sophia felt called to missions in Africa. Her only hesitancy was that she had a deep desire to be married and she knew that where she was going, she was very unlikely to meet an eligible young man who loved the Lord. But she surrendered that desire and heeded the call, going to a dry and dusty land in the heart of Africa to befriend Muslim women and children.

There, to her great delight, she met the man of her dreams. He too had come as a missionary. They developed a strong friendship and were, as Sophia says, "so good to-gether"! They were both cautious about plunging in too quickly, each seeking the Lord and godly counsel. When the lights all seemed green, they moved ahead to see if God was calling them into marriage. Sophia traveled to England to meet his family, and he came to America to meet hers. It was a joyful, exciting time.

Then he began to have doubts, uncertainties about issues in his life. He opened up to Sophia about them. They discussed them together, and though he was kind and so sad to be bringing her this pain, Sophia realized his conflict was deep and she needed to release him. He flew home to England, an ocean between them, leaving Sophia with shattered dreams, sobbing on her mother's couch.

When Sophia shared her story at our community's Christmas Tea for women, I know some were waiting for the happy chick-flick ending in which God brings this young man to his senses and he returns to America, running to Sophia in the rain, en-gulfing her in his arms, pleading with her to be his wife, and promising to cherish her forever.

There is a happy ending, but it isn't that.

Sophia decided not to return to Africa. Instead she took a job for the tourist season at a resort in my corner of the world: Door County, Wisconsin. She hoped to rest, heal, and get some answers from God. She lamented,

- *How could You let this happen, God?*
- *We tried so hard to hear from You—to do it right!*
- *Your Word says not to awaken love before the time is right, and I obeyed that!*
- *I know You aren't a God who plays tricks, but I feel like You led me on!*

Sophia was being honest with God. And that's when the dialogue began to open— she neither heard a voice from heaven nor saw a vision, but He came to her in ordinary ways.

## Arise, My Love

One day Sophia came across Sara Hagerty's book *Every Bitter Thing Is Sweet*. Sophia thought, *Could something sweet really come out of my pain?* She read Sara's own story of heartbreak—of physical barrenness, though Sara believed strongly she was called to motherhood. God began to bring healing to Sara, as she lamented and pressed into Him for help. And He met Sara, speaking to her gently through His Word, His Spirit, and His family. She surrendered her dream to Him, and He gave her a different dream.

Sara and her husband began to adopt one child after another, each one bringing his or her own remarkable story of God's faithfulness. And then, when their home was brimming with beautiful children, Sara and her husband discovered they were expecting a son . . . and then a daughter—two unexpected babies to complete their family of eight.

The greatest change in Sara, though, was not in her circumstances but in her sense of the presence of the Lord and in discovering that in His presence is fullness of joy. It was an awareness that she would say came not in spite of her pain but because of it.

Sophia followed Sara's model in endeavoring to release her dream and in not backing away from God but pressing in to Him. She found herself drawn to the Song of Songs, that mysterious book of earthly love that points, as all the Old Testament books do, to Christ. He is the Bridegroom hidden in the earthly bridegroom who rejoices over his bride.

Sophia was particularly captivated by the second chapter of the Song of Songs, where the bridegroom proposes to the bride, saying,

Arise, my love, my beautiful one,
   and come away,
for behold, the winter is past;
   the rain is over and gone. . . .
Arise my love, my beautiful one,
   and come away.
   —verses 10–11, 13

When a friend suggested she read the second chapter of the Song of Songs, not knowing Sophia already was, Sophia knew confirmation in her desire to be with Jesus, allowing Him to meet her.

One day Sophia showed *Every Bitter Thing Is Sweet* to Whitney, a friend at church. Whitney turned the book over and saw an endorsement from me. She told Sophia that I lived in Door County and that I had a new book out on the Song of Songs called *He Calls You Beautiful*. Another confirmation from God that she needed to understand the message of the Song of Songs.

One Sunday I happened to visit Sophia's church and sat right behind her. During the greeting time, I introduced myself to her and she gave me the widest grin and her eyes filled with tears, for it was yet another confirmation of God's mindfulness of her. When she explained her tears, I invited her and Whitney to my weekly study of the book, and they eagerly accepted.

Through the truths in the Song, God showed Sophia His deep love for her. More and more, she sensed Him rejoicing over her as a bridegroom rejoices over his bride.

One day in our study Sophia shared, "When you give your heart to a man," cupping her hands together as if holding her fragile heart, "it's a real risk, for he may take it and break it. But when you give your heart to the Lord, you can trust Him completely, for He is altogether good and will only do what is best for you, even if it may not at first make sense. He has come to me in a way I did not even imagine was possible. He is filling my life with the joy of His presence."

I can *see* this joy in Sophia, spreading like sunshine wherever she is. People are drawn to her, or in reality, they are drawn to the Jesus in her. She tells me, and I believe her, that she has never known that the love of Jesus could be so *overwhelmingly real*.

## A Love Song

Why am I telling you *this* story in the section on the book of Psalms? Because we are closing with Psalm 45, which is a love song, a royal wedding song—and the Song of Songs in a nutshell.

In the last two years of his life, Jonathan Edwards, that Puritan of such great intellect, wrote extensively in his journals on the parallels between Psalm 45 and the Song of Songs. Since the book of Hebrews clearly tells us that Psalm 45 is about Christ (see Hebrews 1:8–9), that makes a strong case for its counterpart, the Song of Songs, to be, as Edwards put it, "no common love song or epithalamium" but rather a love story that points to the best love story of all: that of Christ for His bride.[1]

I pray that as you see how deep Christ's love is for you, it will help you be true to Him, for better or for worse, in sickness and in health, and for richer or for poorer, until death brings you into His arms forever.

Before we begin, I want to acknowledge that the bridegroom metaphor is more challenging for men. Men can relate to Jesus being their Good Shepherd, the Friend who is closer than a brother, and the Father who cherishes His children—but to the Bridegroom?

I was talking to one group of men about a kiss from the King (Song of Songs 1:2), and one man rolled his eyes and quipped, "Dee, I think I'll take a hug."

And yet, just as we are *all* sons of God (and there is such beauty in realizing that, in Christ, women receive the same inheritance that once was given only to sons), we are *all* also the bride of Christ. The royal Bridegroom of the Song and Psalm 45 is not just coming back for women! And indeed, there is such beauty here for men, too, if they are not so sexualized that they are blinded to the heart of this metaphor: that they are as cherished by God as a new bride is cherished by her husband.

## A Heart Bursting Its Banks

Not very often do the Scriptures give us a peek into how divine inspiration works, but we have a glimpse here, in the opening of Psalm 45:

> My heart bursts its banks,
>     spilling beauty and goodness.
> I pour it out in a poem to the king,
>     shaping the river into words.
>     —verse 1, MSG

This excitement that comes when God illumines us with the truth of His deep love for us cannot help but burst outward, like a river overflowing its banks. That's what I saw happening in the lives of the women in prison when they first studied the Song of Songs. We were filming the curriculum for *He Calls You Beautiful* in a Texas prison, where my publisher had donated three hundred copies to women ahead of the filming.

As part of the filming, we heard testimonies from a few of the women about what they had learned from the Song. Lucy was the first to come up, not being able to contain her enthusiasm. Lucy is a darling, with a tender and teachable heart. Her shiny black locks frame a fair face and a smile that makes you smile! As Lucy took the microphone I handed her, she was trembling from nervous excitement. But her sisters cheered her on, with nods and smiles and an occasional "Amen, sister!"

Lucy began by explaining how God caught her interest immediately when she learned that the Song of Songs means the very best song. So she prayed, *Okay, what do I gotta learn here, Jesus? What do I gotta learn?* What a difference an eager heart makes in our time with the Lord! One of the first questions she tackled was, How do the metaphors that God gives us of Shepherd, Friend, Father, and Bridegroom escalate in intimacy? Lucy's heart "[burst] its banks" as she stood in front of her sisters in Christ sharing, often shedding happy tears, as she described her discovery of God as a Shepherd who protects us, a Friend who holds nothing from us, a Father who loves and disciplines us, and finally a Bridegroom who rejoices over us.

> I'm sitting there on my bunk and picturing all these metaphors in my
> mind. . . . I've never been married, I've never walked down the aisle, I never
> wore a wedding dress . . . but I could imagine it. I closed my eyes and thought
> about how I would feel wearing the dress, walking down the aisle and seeing
> the person I'm going to be with forever—loving him, holding him, and he
> loves me the same. I could picture the butterflies I would feel. Of course
> every woman is going to feel that way on her wedding day—it's her wedding
> day—it's a special day. But then I realized God doesn't just see us that way on
> our wedding day; He sees us like that every day! At that moment, I thought,
> *Oh God—You love us so much that You feel butterflies every time You see us.*
> *You don't look at our past; You look at our heart and You see the beautiful in*
> *each of us. . . . And even if we had a bad wedding day or a bad marriage, we*
> *can visualize that good marriage with You.*

Psalm 45 concentrates just on the wedding to our Bridegroom, but with the help of the Song of Songs, we know much preceded this wedding. The bridegroom had to awaken the bride from her death sleep, to help her see both her sin and his grace, and then lead her through the wilderness to test and refine her. It is in the wilderness that she realizes that all the false gods she has run to failed her and that what she truly needs is only him!

In the Song, the maiden has refused his proposal, fearing commitment, and he has gone away. It is then that she, like the younger prodigal son, comes to her senses and goes out looking for the one "whom my soul loves" (3:2). When she finds him, she will not let him go—and *then,* we have the royal wedding.

## The Most Excellent of Men

In the Song of Songs 5:10, she calls her bridegroom the fairest of ten thousand. Psalm 45 calls him "the most excellent of men" (verse 2, NIV). In the Song she says, "His lips are lilies, dripping liquid myrrh" (5:13). The psalmist says, "Grace is poured upon your lips" (45:2). When Jesus was on earth, people said, "No one ever spoke like this man!" (John 7:46).

He comes for His bride like a warrior ready to do battle. In the Song, he comes with sixty mighty men, all wearing swords. In Psalm 45, he rides out in majesty, with a sword on his thigh and sharp arrows for the hearts of the enemies. Both remind me of the picture in Revelation 19 when Jesus comes on a white horse to do battle with the enemies of His bride: out of His mouth comes a sharp sword, and all the armies of heaven are following Him on white horses (verses 11–16).

Right now, we live in enemy territory, where we face sin, sickness, persecution, death, and Satan himself—but one day all that will be gone, for the King is coming back. John tells us that Christ came to destroy the works of the devil, and when He returns, when we see Him as He is, we will become like Him. John says, "Everyone who thus hopes in him purifies himself as he is pure" (1 John 3:3). One day all sin and sadness will be gone, there will a new heaven and a new earth, and we will know a joy like we have only tasted on earth—and it will last forever.

But to live in this story well, we must be confident of Christ's love for us. How is it possible that we, who are so sinful, can be so cherished?

In the wedding in the Song, the groom is perfumed with frankincense and myrrh, a most unusual fragrance for a bridegroom. Likewise, the bridegroom of Psalm 45 had robes fragrant with myrrh.

Author and professor Michael Reeves explains that frankincense was used in the incense that burned in the temple, and myrrh was used to anoint bodies. Basically, "the King arrives for his wedding day smelling like a dead high priest waving incense."[2] How strange—unless you realize that this symbolizes how Christ, our High Priest, died that we might be cleansed and beautiful in His sight.

If my confidence in God's love rests on my goodness, I am standing on a house of cards. But if my confidence in His love rests on His grace, then I stand on solid rock, as sure of His unfailing love each morning as I am that the sun will rise. And if we are sure of His love, not in just an intellectual sense but with all our hearts and souls, then we *will* "forget [our] people and [our] father's house," as the psalmist writes in verse 10. What does this mean?

## Reshaping Our Greatest Desire

In the Song, the bridegroom asks the maiden to come away with him. Likewise, in Psalm 45, he asks her to leave her father and mother and cleave to him.

As in earthly marriage, this doesn't mean that we abandon our families but that we now have a new priority. Spiritually speaking, this means we first seek Christ and His righteousness all through the day. As the Westminster Catechism tells us, our chief end is to glorify God and enjoy Him forever.

As A. W. Tozer observed, being set free from the power of sin happens to those whose *predominant* desire is to glorify God.[3] Those believers experience a joy and a freedom that believers who cling to other things can never know. Fear keeps those believers caged like timid birds who won't fly out of their cages to freedom when the doors are opened.

As we learned in Psalm 16:4, "the sorrows of those who run after another god shall multiply." Recently when studying heart idols, one young woman told me, "I don't like this study. I want to be happy and this is making me unhappy." Seeing and relinquishing our heart idols does feel painful initially, but Jesus promises, "If you cling to your life, you will lose it; but if you give up your life for me, you will find it" (Matthew 10:39, NLT).

The metaphor of marriage is illuminating, for we do give up independence to be one with our spouse, but we do it for love and are glad (usually) we did. How much more treasure is there to be found when we give up our independence to be one with the absolutely perfect Bridegroom!

## Jesus Is Returning for His Bride

Do we *really* believe Jesus is coming back? Or are we like the virgins in the parable Jesus tells who were not prepared when He returned (Matthew 25:1–13)?

We see the promise of Christ's return throughout the Old Testament. Both Psalm 45 and Song of Songs show a great wedding day when Christ comes for His bride. Likewise, both Song of Songs and the book of Revelation end with the bride calling for her groom to return. Here it is in the Song:

Make haste, my beloved,
and be like a gazelle
or a young stag
on the mountains of spices.
—8:14

Revelation ends with "the Spirit and the Bride say[ing], 'Come,'" and then John closing with "Amen. Come, Lord Jesus!" (22:17, 20). Charles Spurgeon noted that "the Song of love [the Song of Songs] and the Book of love [the Bible] end in almost the selfsame way, with a strong desire for Christ's speedy return."[4]

But it is through the prophets that we see the clearest predictions of Christ's return. We are going to turn, for the last section of this book, to the prophet Isaiah, for this is where Christ turned when He began His ministry.

Come and feast on the grandeur of Isaiah.

## Bible Study Ten

As a group, view the related video and share comments: go to deebrestin.com and click on The Jesus Who Surprises under Free Teaching Videos. Also, as an option for going deeper, listen online to "Enjoying Christ Constantly" by Mike Reeves.

### Week Ten God Hunt

This week look for and record a "kiss from the King": an unexpected encounter that makes you suspect God is behind it, a verse or idea that you hear several times from different sources, an answer to prayer, or His peace despite circumstances.

### Day One: Chapter Review

1. Read the chapter and highlight as you read. Write down two thoughts that impressed you and share one with the group.

2. If you listened to "Enjoying Christ Constantly" by Mike Reeves, what do you remember?

*Today I spied God when . . .*

## Day Two: My Heart Is Stirred

3. Read Psalm 45 in its entirety for an overview.

   a. How would you summarize the theme of this psalm in a sentence?

   b. Did any verses become radioactive to you? If so, why?

*4. In verse 1, we're given some insight into how holy men inspired by God wrote the Scriptures. What do you see?

5. Read Hebrews 1:8–9, where Psalm 45 is quoted. Who does the author of Hebrews say this psalm describes?

*Today I spied God when . . .*

## Day Three: Grace and Truth from This Royal Bridegroom

6. What thoughts do you have that might help men (or you, if you are a man) relate to the metaphor of the Bridegroom?

7. Read Psalm 45:2–5 and list some of the phrases that describe Jesus, the Bridegroom, here.

8. In the Song of Songs 5:13, we are told that "his lips are lilies, dripping liquid myrrh," and here in this psalm, verse 2, we are told, "Grace is poured upon your lips." Jesus is also called, by John, "the Word" (1 John 1:1, NIV). How has Jesus, the Word of God, given you grace? Give a specific example.

9. We live in a world that is enemy territory. Satan is the prince of this world and brings great sorrow. But one day Jesus is returning. Write what you learn from the following passages about our enemy's fate. And why.

   a. Psalm 45:4–5

   b. Song of Songs 3:7–8 (The earthly picture of Solomon points to the great wedding day when Christ returns for His bride.)

c. Revelation 19:11–16

10. Read Psalm 45:1–9.

   a. In verse 1, the psalmist says he is addressing verses to his king.
      What does he call this king in verses 6–7?

   b. How long will this new and coming kingdom last, and what do
      you learn about it from this passage?

   c. In Song of Songs 3:6, the bridegroom is perfumed with frankin-
      cense and myrrh. What similarity do you see in Psalm 45:8? Since
      myrrh is associated with death, what significance do you see in this
      bridegroom's fragrance?

*Today I spied God when . . .*

## Day Four: All Glorious Is the Bride

11. Read Psalm 45:10–12.

   a. Do any verses stand out to you? If so, why?

   b. In the Song of Songs, the bride is called a "noble daughter" (7:1).
      How do you also see her described as royalty in Psalm 45:10–15?




*c. What does the bridegroom ask her to do in response to him in verse
    10? What do you think this means and why?




   d. In what ways have you, by faith, died to yourself or to this world in
      order to glorify your King?




12. Psalm 45:13–15 describes the bride. In verse 13, some translations speak
    of "her chamber," but actually that phrase is not there in the Hebrew. The
    New American Standard Bible (NASB) offers a more accurate translation
    of this verse: "The King's daughter is all glorious within; her clothing is
    interwoven with gold." Puritan Jonathan Edwards felt the plainest
    meaning is that just as the bride's clothing was beautiful, so the parts
    of her body hidden by her clothing were beautiful. Repeatedly Scripture
    affirms the beauty of the marriage bed. On an earthly level, both love
    songs in Scripture (the Song of Songs and Psalm 45) also affirm this.
    What do you learn from the following about how God views sex as He
    created it to be?

    a. Hebrews 13:4

b. Proverbs 5:15–23

c. Song of Songs 4:9–16

d. Psalm 45:13

13. How does God's view of the marriage bed impact you personally?

*Today I spied God when . . .*

## Day Five: Oh Glorious Day

Today we will ponder this most intimate of metaphors and the closing of Psalm 45.

14. The love song of Psalm 45, the Song of Songs, Revelation, the parables, and the prophets all liken our relationship to Christ as a bride to her husband. On a spiritual level, write how each of the following metaphors for God escalate in intimacy: Shepherd, Friend, Father, and Bridegroom. (Lucy, in her testimony, answers this!)

15. Consider the following aspects of marriage and how they might relate, on a spiritual level, to the believer's relationship with Christ:

   a. Faithfulness

   b. Purity

   c. Passion

16. The "bride" in both the Song of Songs and Psalm 45 is both individual and corporate. We *are* loved as individuals, yet how beautiful is the body of Christ, made up of every tribe and nation. In the following, how do you see the corporate nature of the bride of Christ?

   a. Psalm 45:9

   b. Psalm 45:14

17. In verses 16–17, the *your* and *you* are masculine, for the psalmist is again turning his attention to the King. What is God the Father telling God the Son here that will help Him lay down His life for His bride? (*Sons* here refers to both men and women, for we are all "sons" of God just as we are all the "bride of Christ.")

18. What is your takeaway for this week and why?


*Today I spied God when . . .*


## Prayer Time

Spend time in both praise and petition. Divide into small groups if your group is large.

# PART THREE

# How the Story Will End

## The Prophets

# ELEVEN

# Holy, Holy, Holy

## First, We Must Be Undone

> If ever there was a man of integrity, it was Isaiah ben
> Amoz. . . . Then he caught one sudden glimpse of a holy
> God. In that single moment, all of his self-esteem was
> shattered. In a brief second he was exposed, made naked
> beneath the gaze of the absolute standard of holiness.
>
> —R. C. SPROUL

About a year after I came to Christ, Steve did as well. We were both *so* surprised at the
sheer relief we felt, for we had not realized how heavy had been the burden of sin we were
carrying. But oh my, we knew it when it was gone!

At one of those early Christmases we celebrated as believers, we searched for a card
to express our overwhelming joy to friends and family. I found a card with a picture of
a bright-red cardinal perched on new-fallen snow. I showed it to Steve and suggested we
have the following verse from Isaiah printed inside:

> Come now, let us reason together, says the LORD:
> though your sins are like scarlet,
>     they shall be as white as snow.
> —1:18

Steve said, "That is such a great picture of both the bad news and the good news of
the gospel." We decided I would add a handwritten sentence saying how thankful we

were to have our sins forgiven. We mailed out about one hundred cards, oblivious to the storm we would unleash.

One of my Christian friends told me, "Dee, the residents' wives are really offended by the card you sent." (Steve was doing his medical residency in orthopedic surgery.) My heart chilled as she told me the questions they were asking one another:

"What are Steve and Dee accusing us of?"

"What *scarlet* sins do they think we have?"

"Just who do they think they are?"

We were regretful, for our friends had interpreted our testimony as a missile of accusation. If God hadn't brought us into His blazing light, we might have reacted exactly the same way. My stuttered attempts at apologies and explanations were met with cool silence.

Of course. Until I came into the presence of our holy God, I didn't realize how sinful I was. And yet, as Isaiah says, we are *all* unclean, and even "our righteous acts are like filthy rags" (64:6, NIV). Even a man like Isaiah, whom R. C. Sproul says was "considered by his contemporaries as the most righteous man in the nation,"[1] was unclean. Before God could use him as a prophet to Israel, Isaiah had to be humbled, to see himself in the light of a God who is holy, holy, holy.

## Isaiah's Commission

Isaiah experiences the mysterium tremendum when he sees the Lord sitting on a throne, high and lifted up, with the train of His robe filling the temple. Seraphim with six wings (two covering their eyes, two covering their feet, and two flying) are singing,

> Holy, holy, holy is the LORD of hosts;
> the whole earth is full of his glory!
> —6:3

Then the foundations of the threshold shake and the temple is filled with smoke. Isaiah cries out,

> Woe is me for I am ruined
> because I am a man of unclean lips

and live among a people of unclean lips,

and because my eyes have seen the King,

the LORD of Hosts.

—6:5, HCSB

Ruined! The King James Version says "undone"! And the first thing Isaiah is aware of is his mouth, his "unclean lips." Why? Perhaps it is because, as Jesus says, the overflow of our lips reveals what is in our hearts. It may seem like a small matter, for example, to complain, but it reveals a heart that does not trust the sovereignty of God. When sarcasm flows from our mouth, it is the overflow of a heart that festers with bitterness.

When Isaiah stands before a God who is holy, holy, holy, he sees his sin and unravels. If you have ever been with someone who is having a panic attack, you know she feels like her innards are coming apart and that death is imminent. I believe that is how Isaiah is feeling. But then one of the seraphim flies to him, puts a hot coal to those guilty lips, and pronounces, "Behold, this has touched your lips; your guilt is taken away, and your sin atoned for" (6:7).

*Now* Isaiah is fit to go and tell God's people of their sin.

All of the prophets speak against the sin of God's people. So why am I singling out Isaiah to represent the prophets' section of this book? It is to Isaiah that Jesus first turns when He begins His ministry on earth. He unrolls the scroll of Isaiah and quotes the prophecy that God is sending a Messiah to "proclaim good news to the poor . . . liberty to the captives . . . [and] sight to the blind" (Luke 4:18, quoting Isaiah 61:1). When He finishes, He says, "Today this Scripture has been fulfilled in your hearing" (Luke 4:21).

And I suspect it is to Isaiah 53 that Jesus turns at the end of His ministry on earth, when He opens the Scriptures to the two on the road to Emmaus, for He has just fulfilled, to the letter, Isaiah's prophecy of the Messiah's future crucifixion and resurrection.

By the time we get to Isaiah 53, the good news of the gospel is flowing from this prophet, leading to some astounding prophecies about heaven. I can hardly wait to show you just how wonderful it will be and how different from what many of us have imagined! But before we get to the good news, we must see that the first two-thirds of Isaiah is very *bad* news for God's people.

Isaiah begins in a courtroom. To gain perspective on just why God was so angry with His people and why He was going to discipline them so severely, I want to take you to a contemporary courtroom.

# "I Pray You Experience the Soul-Crushing Weight of Guilt"

Larry Nassar, once a world-renowned sports physician, was sentenced to 175 years in prison after two hundred women who were once young Olympic gymnasts testified that he sexually molested them. The first to publicly accuse him, giving courage to a flood of other victims, was Rachael Denhollander. When she testified, she did so with such eloquence and grace that excerpts from her forty-five-minute testimony were broadcast around the world and then went viral on the Internet. Indeed, I believe Denhollander was filled with the Spirit of our holy and just God.

Like the other gymnasts, some as young as six when molested, Denhollander expressed how Nassar had premeditated the abuse, displayed an outward persona that caused adults to trust him, and repeatedly molested her. Like the other victims, she explained how this had destroyed her innocence and haunted her life. But then Denhollander brought the gospel to Nassar, in a manner similar to the way Isaiah brought the gospel to rebellious Israel. She showed both the ferocious consequences of truth and judgment and also the enormity of God's grace to the truly repentant. Here are excerpts from Denhollander's stirring courtroom address:

> You spoke of praying for forgiveness. But Larry, if you have read the Bible you carry, you know forgiveness does not come from doing good things, as if good deeds can erase what you have done. It comes from repentance which requires facing and acknowledging the truth about what you have done in all of its utter depravity and horror without mitigation, without excuse. . . .
>
> The Bible you carry says it is better for a stone to be thrown around your neck and you throw[n] into a lake than for you to make even one child stumble. And you have damaged hundreds.
>
> The Bible you speak [sic] carries a final judgment where all of God's wrath and eternal terror is poured out on men like you. Should you ever reach the point of truly facing what you have done, the guilt will be crushing. And that is what makes the gospel of Christ so sweet. Because it extends grace and hope and mercy where none should be found. And it will be there for you.

I pray you experience the soul-crushing weight of guilt so you may someday experience true repentance and true forgiveness from God, which you need far more than forgiveness from me—though I extend that to you as well.

Throughout this process, I have clung to a quote by C. S. Lewis, where he says, my argument against God was that the universe seems so cruel and unjust. But how did I get this idea of just, unjust? A man does not call a line crooked unless he first has some idea of straight. What was I comparing the universe to when I called it unjust?

Larry, I can call what you did evil and wicked because it was. And I know it was evil and wicked because the straight line exists.[2]

As we move into Isaiah's courtroom, Isaiah holds up this "straight line" of our holy God, for before we can appreciate just how beautiful the gospel is, we must see how desperately we need forgiveness. Like Isaiah, we need to be undone.

## Isaiah's Courtroom

The preface of Isaiah contains three charges against God's people. The Bible is remarkable in that, though Isaiah lived over seven hundred years before Christ's first coming, this courtroom message, and indeed all of Isaiah, is just as relevant to God's people today as it was then. We could be in that same courtroom, hearing the same charges of iniquity, insincerity, and injustice.

### Charge 1: Iniquity

The first charge God must make against His own children is that they have rebelled. Sin, or iniquity, is rebelling against the straight line of God. This straight line, as C. S. Lewis points out, is known intuitively by every person. Yet it is also true that we can suppress that God-given conscience so that we can go our own way, which is exactly what God says has happened to His people. Even an ox and a donkey are more sensitive to their master than are God's people:

The ox knows its owner,
   and the donkey its master's crib,

but Israel does not know,

> my people do not understand.
> —Isaiah 1:3

## Charge 2: Insincerity

Larry Nassar put on a caring persona, charming the parents of his victims to gain access to their children. Then when he was brought into court, he carried his Bible, as if he were a man who did what was right.

Likewise, God's people are still going to the temple, still sacrificing lambs, but their hearts are far from God. What a stench this is to God! Hear His disgust and outrage:

> I have had enough of burnt offerings of rams. . . .
> Your new moons and your appointed feasts
>
> > my soul hates.
> > —Isaiah 1:11, 14

> This people draw near with their mouth
>
> > and honor me with their lips,
> > while their hearts are far from me.
> > —Isaiah 29:13

We need to take His holiness seriously and, as Rachael Denhollander put it, "experience the soul crushing weight of guilt" so that we will *truly* repent and experience the power, joy, and transformation that come with God's forgiveness.

Twenty-five times in Isaiah God is called "the Holy One of Israel." In Him is no darkness at all, and coming into His searing light is like suddenly flipping on the lights in a basement and seeing the rats scurry away. They were there all the time—we just didn't know it until the light revealed them.

## Charge 3: Injustice

Jesus calls us to be like a city on the hill, shining light into the darkness. And indeed the body of Christ has often been that, going where unbelievers do not go: into the plagues of cholera and Ebola; fighting against slavery, the sex trade, hunger, and the slaughter of innocents. They have brought the gospel into prisons and pagan lands, established orphanages and hospitals around the world, and been the heart and hands of Christ to the forgotten.

Despite all that Christians have accomplished, we have also failed miserably. I remember the first time I heard someone preach on Isaiah 58. (It was a sermon by Greg Scharf, the same pastor who, twenty-five years later, invited our daughter Sally to live with his family after Steve died.) Pastor Scharf said that Isaiah was describing a people who were going through the motions—going to religious services and even fasting. Yet Isaiah proclaimed, "On the day of your fasting, you do as you please" (verse 3, NIV). They were putting on an appearance of godliness yet simultaneously shutting their eyes to those in need. *How often,* I thought, *have I shut up my heart to those in need so that I could avoid discomfort?*

My pastor continued, and God's Word continued to be a sword to my soul:

Is not this the fast that I choose . . . ?
Is it not to share your bread with the hungry
    and bring the homeless poor into your house . . . ?
—verses 6–7

"We can't do it all," Pastor Scharf said, "but we must do something. We must keep our heart and eyes open and He *will* guide us. Ruthie [his wife] and I have found one of the best ways to respond to a needy world is to simply have someone in need move in with us."

Steve and I were convicted. This sermon led to our first overseas adoption and to many individuals living with us for months or even years. Still, I have an ongoing struggle with the temptation to shut up my compassion when God brings someone across my path who is lonely, grieving, or just plain challenging. I know that if I close my eyes to those in need and to the Lord's light, it leads me down a path of increasing darkness (1 John 2:11), but if I respond, I experience the validity of Isaiah's promise "Your light [shall] break forth like the dawn" (Isaiah 58:8).

The opening to Isaiah shows us that individual sin leads to cultural breakdown. Every time an individual chooses the darkness out of self-interest, that person's blindness increases. In Denhollander's address, she told how many times she tried to get help from authorities but they protected Nassar. Closing their eyes to her need, they themselves became blind.[3]

I have witnessed this deafness and blindness in my own country of America—what would have been considered grievous or even abhorrent when I was a child is accepted today. Take *just* the example of what has happened because individuals demanded sexual freedom: since *Roe v. Wade* in 1973, sixty million babies have been aborted (ten times the number of lives lost in the Holocaust), sexually transmitted diseases and gender confusion are rampant, marriage has broken down, and many leaders molest the children and women under their power. Individual sin leads to cultural breakdown, and it is usually women and children who suffer the most:

> How the faithful city
> > has become a whore,
> > she who was full of justice!
> Righteousness lodged in her,
> > but now murderers. . . .
> They do not bring justice to the fatherless,
> > and the widow's cause does not come to them.
> —Isaiah 1:21, 23

Do our individual choices matter in bringing justice to others? Yes, for our choices affect our character, our health, and our vision! The effects of our private choices ripple out and touch the lives of others.

## We Are God's Vineyard

In my little corner of the world, I have been a part of a new church plant we named the Orchard. We named it that in part because this thumb of Wisconsin is abundant with cherry orchards but primarily because God uses pictures of healthy fruit trees and vineyards in Scripture to represent what He longs to see in His children. He wants each of us to abide in Christ, the vine, so that *together* we become a picture of a fruitful orchard or vineyard.

But so often, we fail Him. This is what we see in the close of the preface to Isaiah, when God examines the vineyard He cared for with such diligence and tenderness and laments,

What more was there to do for my vineyard,
    that I have not done in it?
When I looked for it to yield grapes,
    why did it yield wild grapes?
—Isaiah 5:4

One of the things that causes my heart to burn within me when I read Scripture is to see that though there are sixty-six books written by many men, from many cultures, over many centuries, often with no contact with one another, still the Bible is just *one* story, *one* seamless tapestry. Take this illustration of the vineyard. The vineyard is a prominent picture throughout the Old Testament. God wanted vineyards to be fruitful and for the owners to share the bounty with widows and sojourners. He also repeatedly used it as a picture of believers.

For example, three hundred years before Isaiah, we see a picture of a vineyard in the Song of Songs. In this Song, the bride keeps referring to herself as a vineyard. In the opening, she is ashamed of her vineyard and pleads with the bridegroom/king not to gaze on her because "my own vineyard I have not kept!" (1:6). Yet, this bridegroom convinces her of his great love for her, wooing her, winning her, and wedding her. By the end of the Song, her vineyard is bursting with beautiful fruit and she is eager for him to see it.

All this ties together when Jesus, a thousand years later, says, "I am the vine; you are the branches. Whoever abides in me and I in him, he it is that bears much fruit, for apart from me you can do nothing" (John 15:5).

Unlike other world religions, which are mechanical, Christianity is organic. We are not to strive to muster up fruit in our own strength, or staple it on in pretense, but instead we are called to simply abide in Christ. Then His life will flow through us and burst with all the fruit of the Spirit.

But God's people were not abiding in Isaiah's day, just as we often fail to abide in our day. So God tells them, through Isaiah, that He is coming with His pruning shears and it is going to hurt terribly.

And just as in Isaiah's day, there are some who struggle to believe this today. They feel that God is only a God of mercy, not of judgment, and they cannot accept these passages of the Bible.

## Holiness Demands Justice

I know many people who cannot accept a God of judgment. Either they have not read the Bible carefully, or they dismiss those passages as myths, metaphors, or mistakes. They feel a God of judgment is incompatible with a God of love.

Miroslav Volf, the Croatian theologian from Yale, says the Western world, in our comfortable suburban homes, shuns a God of justice. The people in his ravaged homeland feel differently. Volf asks us to imagine giving that message of a grace-only God to people in a war zone: "Among your listeners are people whose cities and villages have been first plundered, then burned and leveled to the ground, whose daughters and sisters have been raped, whose fathers and brothers have had their throats slit."[4]

Indeed, love is not love if it is only grace. That is enablement. How can it be loving to let the perpetrators of rape, murder, and persecution go free? As John Eldredge writes, "This is where Hinduism, Buddhism, and other religions that deny or ignore the actual, personal existence of evil fall so short. (Branches of Christianity have done the same.) Without naming evil for exactly what it is, and without a day of reckoning, there can be no justice."[5]

It is Christianity that helps its followers not to take justice into their own hands, for they know God will be just. As Paul admonishes, "Beloved, never avenge yourselves, but leave it to the wrath of God, for it is written, 'Vengeance is mine, I will repay, says the Lord'" (Romans 12:19).

Indeed, after Isaiah has indicted God's people, listing their sins, he tells them of the frightening pruning that is to come. One day the fierce Babylonians will come, destroy Jerusalem, and take God's people captive for seventy years. After that, God will avenge the Babylonians by using the Assyrians. And indeed, all this literally came to pass, just as Isaiah prophesied it would.

Pastor Scharf explains that every judgment we see in Scripture is a foreshadowing of a much worse final judgment. We see as Isaiah's telescope takes in the near and far mountaintops of the impending judgment and also the terrible final judgment, sometimes so merged that we are not sure which time he is seeing.

For example, concerning the oracle against Babylon, the description of its judgment suddenly merges into the description of the final judgment prophesied by Jesus in the Gospels:

The stars of the heavens and their constellations
> will not give their light;
the sun will be dark at its rising,
> and the moon will not shed its light.
> —Isaiah 13:10

In those days, after that tribulation, the sun will be darkened, and the moon will
not give its light, and the stars will be falling from heaven.
> —Mark 13:24–25

Can we trust Isaiah's prophecies concerning the end times? And how literally can
we take them?

## "Ask Me of Things to Come"

No stone god or god of any other religion has been able to predict the future without
error as the biblical prophets have. Indeed, it is *only* the God of Christianity who dares
to say, "Ask me of things to come" (Isaiah 45:11). God has even given us a way to test the
accuracy of someone who claims to be His prophet: "If you say in your heart, 'How may
we know the word that the LORD has not spoken?'—when a prophet speaks in the name
of the LORD, if the word does not come to pass or come true, that is a word that the
LORD has not spoken; the prophet has spoken it presumptuously. You need not be afraid
of him" (Deuteronomy 18:21–22).

So how accurate were Isaiah's mountaintop prophecies?

They were fulfilled to the letter. In 597 BC, King Nebuchadnezzar of Babylon lays
siege to Jerusalem. The people of Judah see their city and the temple destroyed and
thousands slaughtered or taken captive, just as Isaiah has said would happen.

Yet the book of Isaiah, like all of Scripture, has often been the object of attack. There
were those who said that the Isaiah who was commissioned in the year King Uzziah
died (740 BC) could not have written all of this book, for how could he possibly have
known that God's people would be taken captive by the Babylonians one hundred fifty
years later? How could he have named Cyrus as the man who would free them, when
Cyrus had not even been born (Isaiah 45:1–4)? And how could he have possibly de-

scribed the crucifixion of Christ in such accurate detail six hundred years before it actually happened? Some surmised there must have been two or even three Isaiahs and not just one. But Peter explains how Isaiah could have known all this before it actually happened: "No prophecy was ever produced by the will of man, but men spoke from God as they were carried along by the Holy Spirit" (2 Peter 1:21).

Some have said that because scriptural scrolls were copied and recopied, there had to be many errors. Once, our oldest manuscripts of Isaiah were dated shortly after the birth of Christ. But in 1942, manuscripts a thousand years older than anything we had were discovered in caves near Qumran. There were five nearly complete Isaiah manuscripts.

Dr. Catherine McDowell, who teaches Old Testament at Gordon-Conwell, explains the great significance of what have come to be known as the Dead Sea Scrolls:

> The significant continuity between the biblical texts from the Dead Sea Scrolls
> and the medieval Old Testament manuscripts testifies to a scribal tradition that
> was committed to the preservation of the Scripture, and to a God who superin-
> tended the process. There are differences, to be sure, but they constitute only
> about 1 percent of the readings. Thus, we can rest assured that our English
> Bibles are excellent and faithful translations of God's Word.[6]

Isaiah's prophecies are spot on. He tells God's people that the Babylonians are coming to destroy their city, murder, and take their fit youth captive, and it all comes to pass. Rather than go into all these painful prophecies, I am going to fast-forward to their fulfillment, using a lament from one of those captives in Babylon, the psalmist of Psalm 137.

## By the Waters of Babylon

God's people are weeping as they sit by the waters of Babylon, remembering their murdered loved ones, their destroyed city. As Derek Kidner says of Psalm 137, "Every line of it is alive with pain, whose intensity grows with each strophe to the appalling climax."[7]

The tormentors would require their captives to sing, making mirth of their losses, saying, "Sing us one of the songs of Zion!" (verse 3). It reminds me of African slaves

being forced to sing and dance on the slave ships or at the end of a long day. We are told
God's people refused, hanging their lyres on the willow trees and saying,

> How shall we sing the LORD's song
> in a foreign land?
> If I forget you, O Jerusalem,
> let my right hand forget its skill!
> Let my tongue stick to the roof of my mouth,
> if I do not remember you,
> if I do not set Jerusalem
> above my highest joy!
> —verses 4–6

Their intensity and their love for Jerusalem has increased. They now appreciate what
they have lost. What we can see in this psalm is repentance—turning from their idols,
which *had* been their highest joy, to Jerusalem (which is a way of saying "God's kingdom") as their highest joy.

We also see red-hot anger at the close of this psalm, when God's people pray for
justice against their enemies. They had seen their babies dashed against the rocks, and
now they ask the same for the Babylonians. This is a psalm of lament where the psalmist
is being truthful about his real feelings rather than reflecting the heart of God. (But it is
shocking, and we will ponder it together in the Bible study.)

There is *so* much judgment and pain in Isaiah that indeed we are thirsting for the
good news of the gospel by the time we finally get to Isaiah 40. How relieved we are to
finally come to the words that cannot help but bring to our remembrance the wonderful
strains of the opening of Handel's *Messiah:*

> Comfort ye, comfort ye my people, saith your God.
> Speak ye comfortably to Jerusalem, and cry unto her, that her warfare
> is accomplished, that her iniquity is pardoned.
> —verses 1–2, KJV

I'm sure you are ready for the good news, to be comforted by the promises of God,
which are *just* as certain to be literally fulfilled as were His promises of judgment.

**Bible Study Eleven**

Your facilitator may divide this study into two weeks. As a group, view the related video and share comments: go to deebrestin.com and click on *The Jesus Who Surprises* under Free Teaching Videos. Also, as an option for going deeper, listen online to "The Trauma of Holiness" by R. C. Sproul.

## Week Eleven God Hunt

Be alert this week for unexpected grace or timing. For example, you got a warning instead of a ticket; you ran into a friend you'd just been thinking about; you prayed to find lost keys—and there they were! Write down each day these or any other ways you spy God this week.

## Day One: Chapter Review

1. Read the chapter and highlight as you read. Write down two thoughts that impressed you and share at least one with the group.

2. If you listened to R. C. Sproul's talk "The Trauma of Holiness," share your thoughts here.

3. When Jesus begins His ministry, He opens the scroll to Isaiah's prophecy about the coming Messiah, reads it, and then proclaims, "Today this Scripture has been fulfilled in your hearing" (Luke 4:21). Read Isaiah 61:1–2 and answer the following:

   a. Why do you think Jesus's words are so surprising to the people in the synagogue?

    b. How has Jesus been any of these things to you recently? Share
       specifically.

  *c. When Jesus reads from Isaiah, He stops in the middle of a sentence.
     Look in Isaiah 61 and see what He does not read. What is it, and
     why do you think He stops?

*Today I spied God when . . .*

## Day Two: Isaiah's Commission

  4. Describe the scene and the message of the seraphim in Isaiah 6:1–4.

  5. The shaking of the earth is a customary reaction to the Lord's presence. (For
    example, see Exodus 19:18 and Habakkuk 3:3–10.) How did the earth react
    in Matthew 27:51–54? Why?

  6. How does Isaiah respond in Isaiah 6:5? Why do you think that is?

  *7. Jesus says, "Out of the abundance of the heart his mouth speaks" (Luke 6:45).
    What do the things you talk about reveal about your heart, including any sin
    in your heart?

*8. How does God show and speak mercy to Isaiah in Isaiah 6:6–7? How do you see the gospel here?

9. Have you ever experienced a sense of "trauma" due to the holiness of God? Have you then also experienced relief? Explain.

*Today I spied God when . . .*

## Day Three: God's Children in Court

10. Read Isaiah 1:1–3.

    a. Who are God's witnesses, according to verse 2?

    b. When God the Judge looks down from His courtroom bench, whom does He see? Why is this so painful?

    c. What do even stubborn animals know that God's people do not?

11. Read 1 John 3:9. What does John tell us?

12. Because we have "God's seed" (1 John 3:9) in us, we have the power to choose the path of privilege. Yet Isaiah says God's children are choosing the path of sin. In other words, we sin because we want to. When we do, what lie are we believing?

13. God charges His people first with iniquity, or rebelling against God's straight line.

   a. According to Romans 1:18–20, why is God is angry with man?

   *b. God has put His law in every man's heart, for even Abraham, who did not have the law, knew what was right. How do you see this sense of "oughtness" in people's hearts, even if they don't know the Bible? How do you see it in your own heart?

14. Read Isaiah 1:4–9.

   a. What metaphors does God use in verse 6 to show the extent of His people's iniquity?

   b. Where do you tend to rebel against the straight line of God?

15. Read verses 10–17. Why is the people's religion a burden to God? What evidences of insincerity does He see? (For those who wish to go deeper, Isaiah expands on this in Isaiah 58.)

16. Read verse 18 aloud. How does this verse show both the bad news and the good news of the gospel?

17. Read verses 21–23.

   a. How has individual sin spread to affect the whole community?

   b. Why is it that sin, even when done behind closed doors, always affects others?

   c. Think about a way you sinned that ended up hurting others, though that was not your intention. (You don't have to share, but consider.)

*Today I spied God when . . .*

## *Day Four: Isaiah Prophesies Coming Judgments*

Isaiah begins in a courtroom, then we have a flashback in Isaiah 6 to Isaiah's commission, and then, all the way to Isaiah 40, we have prophecies of the coming judgments, with flashes of light promising a coming Messiah.

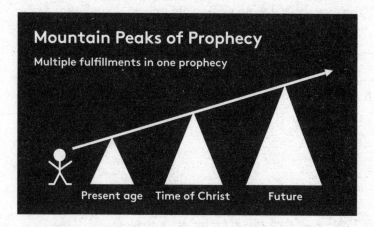

Isaiah sees future events like escalating mountain peaks, the current scene, years ahead to the Babylonian captivity, hundreds of years ahead to Christ's first coming, and then to Christ's second coming. Sometimes these events are mentioned in the same prophecy, for Isaiah does not know *when* these would occur. With only the Second Coming to be fulfilled, we have more clarity.

18. What is the test of a prophet of God, according to Deuteronomy 18:21–22?



19. To illustrate how a near prophecy can also portray a far prophecy, read Isaiah 13:1–11, concerning how God will judge Babylon for its invasion of Judah. How does this passage also allude to a final judgment? (Compare verse 10 with Matthew 24:27–29.)

20. Isaiah gives hope to the people of God concerning a near deliverer and a far deliverer.

   a. Who does Isaiah 45:1 say will one day free the Jews? What was unusual about this conqueror yet to be born, according to verse 4?

   b. Who is the ultimate Deliverer, and what do you learn about Him in Isaiah 9:6–7?

   c. Take one of the above names of Jesus and comment on it. Has He been any of these things to you? If so, explain.

*Today I spied God when . . .*

## Day Five: By the Waters of Babylon

Psalm 137 shows that Isaiah's predictions about Babylon were fulfilled. To prepare your hearts for today, look up Jason Silver singing Psalm 137 on YouTube.

21. What comments do you have on Silver's presentation of Psalm 137?

22. Read verses 1–3 and describe the scene.

23. Read verses 4–6. What evidence of repentance do you see?

24. Read verses 7–9. Describe what the Babylonians did to the Israelites and also what the Israelites ask God to do to the Babylonians.

25. Psalm 137 is both a lamentation and an imprecatory psalm, in which God's people ask God to avenge their enemies. Can you identify with those feelings? What does Romans 12:19 tell us to do with these feelings?

26. Derek Kidner exhorts us to distill the essence of an imprecatory psalm and receive the impact of it so that we might empathize rather than give smooth answers in the face of such pain. But *our* response to cruelty should be to pray for reconciliation, not judgment.[8] What comments do you have on this? Do you believe it is ever appropriate to pray for judgment on an enemy? Why or why not?

27. What is your takeaway this week and why?

*Today I spied God when . . .*

## *Prayer Time*

Cluster in groups of three or four. Using the words of Isaiah 9:6–7, begin with praise. Then, if you are willing, confess sin, either audibly or silently (though James 5:16 encourages us to do it audibly). Then the facilitator will lift up the name of each person and others will support that person.

# Twelve

# Comfort Ye, Comfort Ye, My People

## The Songs of the Servant

In Isaiah 53, "we find ourselves in the presence of love beyond anything known on earth, and the voice which says, 'I was delighted when my Son died for you—and I am still delighted.'"

—J. Alec Motyer

It is not until we get to Isaiah 40, beginning with the words "Comfort ye" (KJV), that the strains of mercy begin to triumph over the strains of judgment.

I cannot read these words without simultaneously hearing Handel's *Messiah* and remembering the times I've heard it performed. It's Advent, and there's excitement as people find their seats in the concert hall. Finally, the lights dim, the crowd hushes, and violins begin their haunting melody. I am transported back to the days of Isaiah, to the people who walked in darkness. Then a sole tenor's voice rises to proclaim,

*Comfort ye. . . . Comfort ye . . . my people . . .*
*Saith your God.*

Handel was said to have written this symphony in three weeks, never leaving his house. A waiter would deliver meals, only to find them untouched. One day he came into the room just as Handel had finished the "Hallelujah Chorus." Handel, tears streaming down his face, said, "I did think I did see all Heaven before me, and the great God Himself."[1]

Performed around the world every Christmas, *The Messiah* continues to turn hearts to God, for it is filled with the very good news of the gospel. And just as I love watching the London Philharmonic or the Boston Symphony perform it, I also love the YouTube videos of flash mobs surprising crowds with the closing "Hallelujah Chorus." In one from 2010, that at this writing has fifty-one million hits,[2] unsuspecting shoppers in a food court are shocked as a young woman in a black jacket and a red Christmas scarf suddenly stands, belting out in clear soprano, *"Hallelujah, Hallelujah, Hallelujah, Hallelujah, Hallelujah."*

People are startled, confused: *What is she doing?* Then a mustached man in a white sweatshirt leaps up onto his chair and echoes with his deep bass, *"Hallelujah, Hallelujah, Hallelujah, Hallelujah, Hallelujah."*

A couple near the rear sing, *"For the Lord God omnipotent reigneth."*

A "janitor" carrying a yellow Caution: Wet Floor sign suddenly turns, lifting his sign as if in praise, and sings, *"Hallelujah, Hallelujah."*

A hush comes over the crowd as they move from confusion to delight and some, particularly the children and the elderly, to awe. More than one hundred choir members are now singing, *"King of kings and Lord of lords. For He shall reign forever and ever."*

The Spirit of God overwhelms this secular scene. Mouths are stopped from chewing and chatter. Souls are stirred as an unseen world comes down, for five marvelous minutes, in the middle of a mall. I think, *Handel's* Messiah, *with its combined power of sacred Scripture, word pictures, and majestic music, has lifted the veil again.*

In the same way, when we get to Isaiah 40, the Spirit of God again brings an abrupt change to the scene, for there is a sharp turn from promised judgment to promised restoration.[3] The people have heard all the terrible things that are going to happen to them, but now they hear that this is *not* the end of the story.

Just as we saw in the previous chapter of this book, Isaiah sees three mountaintops in the future—and though they are separated by centuries, they merge together in one prophecy. But it is all very good news.

Comfort, comfort my people, says your God.
Speak tenderly to Jerusalem,
     and cry to her

that her warfare is ended,
      that her iniquity is pardoned,
that she has received from the LORD's hand
      double for all her sins.
      —verses 1–2

First, on the closest mountaintop, Isaiah sees the end of Israel's warfare and captivity. The people will be released, as they were in the days of Exodus, and nothing, not mountains or seas, can prevent them from getting out:

A voice cries:
"In the wilderness prepare the way of the LORD;
      make straight in the desert a highway for our God.
Every valley shall be lifted up,
      and every mountain and hill be made low;
the uneven ground shall become level,
      and the rough places a plain.
And the glory of the LORD shall be revealed,
      and all flesh shall see it together,
      for the mouth of the LORD has spoken."
      —verses 3–5

But do you see that this is referring not only to a great leader like Moses or Cyrus setting the captives free but also to the One who can set us all free from *every* bond, breaking the chains of sin and sorrow and death? There is a much greater restoration coming. We *know* this is simultaneously a prophecy of Jesus Christ, for Matthew quotes this very passage when John the Baptist comes on the scene to prepare the way for the Messiah.

And then we see the first very clear word picture of Jesus:

He will tend his flock like a shepherd;
      he will gather the lambs in his arms;
he will carry them in his bosom,
      and gently lead those that are with young.
      —verse 11

Because this life is hard, we need to know that, as Matthew Henry says, "the struggle will not last always."[4] It sustains us to know that we have a Shepherd who cares for us and can comfort us.

And now the word pictures begin to tumble, one after another, for the rest of Isaiah. Isaiah is told to "speak tenderly" to God's people (verse 2). The Hebrew phrase "speak tenderly" means "speak to the heart." J. Alec Motyer compares it to "an ardent lover wooing his beloved."[5]

The best lovers use word pictures, for indeed this is the most effective way to speak to the heart. Images bypass the logical left brain and tap into the right brain, which is the side that unleashes our emotions. The lovers in the Song of Songs continually use word pictures: she tells him his very name is like "oil poured out" (1:3), and he tells her she is like "a lily among brambles" (2:2).

So now, in this last third of Isaiah, God "speaks tenderly," with one word picture after another, to bring comfort to His people. That view of restoration takes in the near mountaintop release from captivity in Babylon, the next mountaintop of the first coming of the Messiah, and finally, by the time we get to Isaiah 65, the furthest mountaintop of heaven, when the release from sin, sickness, and sorrow is complete.

Each of these pictures, beginning in Isaiah 42 and reaching their peak in Isaiah 53, reveal a Savior who is close to the brokenhearted and was willing to suffer so that we might be healed. These passages are sometimes called the songs of the Servant. Though the Israelites expected the Messiah to be a mighty warrior (and He *will* one day come like that), He is coming the first time as a servant, One who will lay down His life for His sheep.

Let's look at a few of these pictures that God can use in our lives to speak truth and hope in the midst of trial and temptation.

## A Bruised Reed

So many women in prison suffered so much in childhood and then attached themselves to a man they thought would be their ticket to freedom. Instead, that man often ends up being their ticket to drugs, prostitution, and prison.

When these women first come into prison, they are so bruised and broken. Yet just as Jesus had mercy for the downtrodden when He was on earth, He *still* does. His compassion was constantly welling up: toward the widow whose only son had died; toward the adulteress thrown at His feet; toward the despised, the blind, and the brokenhearted. Indeed,

> A bruised reed he will not break,
> and a faintly burning wick he will not quench.
> —Isaiah 42:3

Though it still takes my breath away, God saw our daughter Beth when she was a baby kicking in her blood, abandoned in a field in Thailand, her little arm severed. But as she says, "I didn't die! God heard me crying and sent someone to find me and rush me to the hospital." Then, after nine years of all kinds of abuse in the orphanage, Beth despaired of ever being in a family, for adoptions for children over the age of ten are very rare. Again, Beth says, "God heard my cry and brought my father-to-be from America to rescue me."

How clearly I remember how God orchestrated this. Three years after we adopted Annie, Steve thought we were called to adopt again, "Only this time," he told me, "I think we are ready for a challenge."

I felt my plate was full, and I *wasn't* ready for a challenge. Yet when Steve asked if I would at least pray about it with him, I couldn't refuse. When we prayed, I heard nothing, but Steve heard "a little girl who was crying."

I said, "I think you might have imagined that."

He said, "Maybe I did. Let's see if the Lord confirms it."

A few days later, we got a call from the social worker who had facilitated the adoption of Annie, our Korean daughter. I hadn't talked to the social worker in three years. She told me about a nine-year-old girl in a Thai orphanage. "She's a beautiful little girl, Dee. She is a fighter, a survivor! I thought of your family when I met her. May I send you her picture?"

When Steve saw her picture, he teared up and said, "This is our daughter."

Though I admit I entered into this challenge with trepidation, I am so thankful for this child, who today is a beautiful woman of God, a wife, and a mother of three very active little children. I marvel watching her diaper a wriggling baby with one arm. Her husband tells me, with a mixture of pride and despair, that he came home one day to find her dragging their sofa upstairs with her one arm. And how I remember the phone call I got from her college speech teacher, who said Beth had brought the whole class to tears as she told how God had rescued her.

I have also seen God reach into nursing homes, to my own mother. In the last five years of her life, she was in a wheelchair with dementia. I visited her almost daily, yet she forgot I had just been there, and each time, it was like Christmas all over again. She'd throw up her arms and cry, "My baby! You've come! How wonderful!"

During Easter of my mother's ninety-third year, my eldest son shared the gospel with her as we had many times before and asked her if she would like to put her trust in Christ.

This time she shocked him by saying, "JR, would you help me?" And he did.

Six months later she was put on hospice, and I was with her that last night. She was vomiting blood, writhing in agony. For hours, I paced the floor, praying. "Oh Jesus, You promised that a bruised reed you would not break and a faintly burning wick you would not quench. Mother is just a baby Christian—this is too much for her—it could break her. Please, Gentle Shepherd, lead her gently home."

Fran, her nurse, came into our room long before her shift was to begin, for God had awakened her and put Mother on her heart. She knelt beside Mother and whispered, "Mrs. Brown. You don't have to be afraid to die. All is forgiven and Jesus is waiting for you with open arms."

Mother quieted, looked up, smiled, and was gone.

A bruised reed he will not break,
  and a faintly burning wick he will not quench.
—Isaiah 42:3

But there is more to melt our hearts. This verse is not just telling us of Christ's tenderness; it is also showing us what it took to accomplish this. The word *bruised*, remember, means a deep wound and is also translated "crushed." This is the same Hebrew word used in Genesis when we are told that Satan will bruise Christ's heel but Christ will bruise Satan's head.

Imagine a slithering poisonous snake coming toward those you love, and the only way you can stop him is to stomp on his head with your bare heel. That will kill him, but first he will bite and poison you and you will die. That's what Christ did for us. In Isaiah 53:5, this same word *bruised* is used again, though it's translated "crushed" in the more modern translations:

> He was pierced for our transgressions;
>     he was crushed for our iniquities,
> upon him was the chastisement that brought us peace,
>     and with his wounds we are healed.

He saw our brokenness and was broken Himself, that we might be healed.

## Can a Mother Forget Her Nursing Child?

I remember when a friend of mine, a young nursing mother, accompanied me to a speaking engagement just an hour away, assuming I'd get her home to her baby by 10 p.m. But driving home, a blizzard forced us to stop, knock on the door of a farmhouse, and spend the night. My friend's rock-hard breasts made her miserable. Could she forget her baby? Hardly! What an apt image God gives us when He promises never to forget us:

> Can a woman forget her nursing child,
>     that she should have no compassion on the son of her womb?
> Even these may forget,
>     yet I will not forget you.
> Behold, I have engraved you on the palms of my hands.
>     —Isaiah 49:15–16

God refers to one of the most powerful connections on earth to describe His connection to us.

My longtime editor, Elisa Stanford, has a fourteen-year-old daughter with Down syndrome who has been suffering intensely for eighteen months with a mysterious metabolic disease that has her hallucinating and yelling through sleepless nights and long days. Every now and then the storm calms and Elisa and her husband see the real Eden, but it is rare. The care for Eden, and the journey to find a solution, is relentless. Yet this is what Elisa wrote:

> We always have tremendous love for Eden—in some ways, more and more, if that's even possible. I feel almost a tangible connection to her, which helps me understand God's connection to us more clearly. And the delight we feel when she smiles at us, strokes our hand, or dances in the kitchen is greater than we have known before.

The only love that is stronger than the love of a mother is Christ's love.

And what does it mean to be engraved on the palms of His hands? The Greek word for *engraved* means formed by an incision with a hammer, a chisel, a spike.

I love Caravaggio's painting known as *The Incredulity of St. Thomas.* Thomas said he would not believe unless he saw Jesus's wounds, and He showed him His side and the palms of His hands. And it is not just Thomas who is looking but the other disciples as well. Oh, how we need to gaze on the wounds so that our hearts know the depth of His love. And then, like Thomas, we cry, "My Lord and my God."

## He Set His Face Like Flint

When we get to Isaiah 50, we have a picture of a servant who was determined to obey His Father, no matter what, as Isaiah begins to prophesy the flogging, the mocking, and the spitting that Jesus would endure *before* He endured the cross. Isaiah tells us the Messiah will "set [his] face like flint" to go through this (verses 6–7, NIV).

Flint is extremely hard. It can even start a fire when struck. Setting his face like flint reminds me of Jane Eyre. Mr. Rochester, whom she deeply loves, asks her to live with him outside of marriage, for he already has a wife, a madwoman who lives in the attic. He pleads with Jane, counting the reasons he loves her, telling her he will care for her. She is tortured by her desire, explaining,

> I was experiencing an ordeal: a hand of fiery iron grasped my vitals. Terrible moment: full of struggle, blackness, burning! Not a human being that ever lived could wish to be loved better than I was loved: and him who thus loved me I absolutely worshipped: and I must renounce love and idol.[6]

Here is how she responds to Mr. Rochester's pleadings:

"Jane, you understand what I want of you? Just promise—'I will be yours, Mr. Rochester.'"

"Mr. Rochester, I will *not* be yours." . . .

"All happiness will be torn away with you. What then is left? . . . Where turn for a companion, and for some hope?"

"Do as I do: trust in God and yourself. Believe in heaven. Hope to meet again there." . . .

"Then you condemn me to live wretched, and to die accursed?" his voice rose.

"I advise you to live sinless, and I wish you to die tranquil."[7]

How foreign this can sound to modern ears that think happiness comes from doing whatever you want and attempting to avoid pain. But that is not the way of our Savior, who set His face like flint to pay for our sin, but He did it for the joy set before Him. He loved His bride and was determined to rescue her.

## Isaiah 53: The Golden Treasure of the Old Testament

Surely Jesus turned to Isaiah 53 on the road to Emmaus, for this chapter is quoted more than any other by the New Testament writers. Isaiah 53 begins with "Who has believed what he has heard from us?" (verse 1). Indeed, the idea that God would suffer, be led like a lamb to the slaughter, and bring healing through His death is strange. C. S. Lewis remarked that one of the reasons he *did* believe in Christianity was because it is nothing anyone would have guessed or made up. "It has just that queer twist about it that real things have."[8]

Isaiah's prophecies are so detailed, even saying that this servant will make his grave with the wicked (Jesus was crucified between two thieves) and with a rich man in his death (Joseph, a rich man from Arimathea, gave Him his tomb).

Certain words in Isaiah 53 might shock us, but it is important that we ponder them to understand. For example, Isaiah prophesies,

It was the will of the LORD to crush him;

he has put him to grief.

—verse 10

How are we to understand this? I have a sister who has been taught from the pulpit of her church that this did not happen, for a father would never ask his son to die. But that reflects a misunderstanding of the Trinity—the Father and the Son were in agreement on this plan in rescuing us. As pastor Kevin DeYoung explains,

The Father did not punish the Son as a helpless victim of cosmic child abuse. The Son *went* to the cross freely and willingly. Likewise, the Son did not appease an angry God as some sort of divine good cop to the Father's divine bad cop. The Father *sent* his Son to the cross freely and willingly. . . . The good news of Good Friday is that the Father did not spare his own Son but gave him up for us all (Rom. 8:32) and that the Son drank the bitter cup of God's wrath for our sakes (Mark 14:36).[9]

But what should melt our hearts like nothing else is this: "Out of the anguish of his soul he shall see and be satisfied" (Isaiah 53:11). Why did God the Father and God the Son agree on this terrible but beautiful plan? Because of love for us! God, in the mystery of the Trinity, came for us, and He was able to bear this suffering because He knew it was not the end of the story. He would suffer terribly and die in anguish, but He would also rise from the dead, and one day He, because of this price, would have a pure bride, His church. We were worth it to the Lord. It pleased God, Father and Son, to do it. And God was able to do it because He knew the end of the story.

In the same way, if we know the end of the story, hope can fill our hearts to set our faces like flint in obedience to God for this short time we have on earth. If Isaiah's prophecies were spot on for the first coming of Christ, will they not also be for the second coming of Christ?

Let's look at what Isaiah's telescope reveals about the end of the story. "'There is no peace,' says the LORD, 'for the wicked'" (48:22). And yet, at the same time, Isaiah tells us that, because of mercy, peace is possible. Though in our minds this happens seven hundred years later, Isaiah speaks of it as if it has already happened:

He was pierced for our transgressions;

    he was crushed for our iniquities;

upon him was the chastisement that brought us peace,

    and with his wounds we are healed.

    —53:5

I want to show you this description of God's people, something that causes my heart to burn within me:

They have abandoned the LORD;

they have despised the Holy One of Israel;

they have turned their backs on Him.

    —1:4 (HCSB)

Later, Isaiah takes the very same description he used to condemn God's people and uses it to exalt the coming Messiah:

He was despised and rejected by men,

    a man of sorrows and acquainted with grief;

and as one from whom men hide their faces

    he was despised, and we esteemed him not.

    —53:3

Do you see?

God's people despised Him, so He let Himself be despised.

God's people abandoned Him, so He let Himself be abandoned.

How did Jesus find the strength to bear our sin and go through this horror? In the midst of His dark suffering, He thought of the joy set before Him, for Isaiah 53:11 tells us, "Out of the travail of his soul he shall see light and be satisfied" (Dead Sea Scroll Version). What was that joy? What was the light that satisfied Him? Us! He was providing the final exodus out of slavery for us; He was providing a way for us to be made whiter than snow; He was gaining for Himself a pure bride.

Amazing love, how can it be?

**Bible Study Twelve**

As a group, view the related video and share comments: go to deebrestin.com and click on *The Jesus Who Surprises* under Free Teaching Videos. Also, as an option for going deeper, listen online to "Can a Mother Forget?" by Tim Keller.

## Week Twelve God Hunt

Be still this week and know that He is God. Be open to hearing from Him after studying Scripture or asking for wisdom or comfort. Be alert. Also be aware of the many other ways you may spy Him. Write down your sightings each day.

## Day One: Chapter Review

1. Read the chapter and highlight as you read. Write down two thoughts that impressed you and share at least one with the group.

2. If you listened to Tim Keller's "Can a Mother Forget?" share what stood out to you.

*Today I spied God when . . .*

## Day Two: Flashes of Light

Although there is much doom and gloom in the first two-thirds of Isaiah, God always provides flashes of light to give His people hope. Babylon was a real nation that took Israel captive and made them slaves, but Babylon also symbolizes Satan and how he still ensnares God's children and makes them slaves. These flashes of hope, therefore, were not just for ancient Israel but also for us. Isaiah 9 tells of a reversal of fortune, and the verbs are in the past tense, for the future is a sure hope, as if it had already happened.

3. Read Isaiah 9:1–3 and describe the reversal of fortune Isaiah sees.

4. Read verses 6–7 aloud and note anything that stands out to you about the One who will reverse this fortune.

5. We will learn much more about heaven next week, but in Isaiah 11:6–10, we get a glimpse of what it will be like. What do you learn from these verses?

6. What else do you see about heaven in Isaiah 25:6–10?

*Today I spied God when . . .*

## Day Three: Word Pictures to Comfort Your Soul

Go to YouTube and see the flash mob singing the "Hallelujah Chorus" (search for "Hallelujah flash mob food court").

7. Have you experienced Handel's *Messiah* in any way? If so, share how it has impacted you.

8. Read Isaiah 40:1–2.

   a. What stands out to you and why?

   b. The firstborn son received a double portion of the inheritance
      (Deuteronomy 21:17; Isaiah 61:7). Here in Isaiah 40:2, what has
      Israel received as the firstborn son? Why might children of God be
      disciplined more severely than children of the devil?

9. Read Isaiah 42:1–4 (a bruised reed).

   a. What do you learn about the first coming of Jesus from these
      verses?

   b. What do the word pictures of verse 3 express?

   c. How have you experienced His gentleness recently? (God Hunt!)

   d. The word *bruised* is the same word that is used in Genesis 3:15 and
      Isaiah 53:5 (though it is translated "crushed"). What does this show
      us about how Christ is able to come to us, as sinners, gently?

10. Read Isaiah 49:15–16 (a mother's love).

    a. What word picture is in verse 16, and how is this meaningful to you?

    *b. What does it mean to be "engraved" on the palms of Christ's hands?

*Today I spied God when . . .*

## Day Four: The Heart of Our Savior

11. Read Isaiah 50:4–7 (his face like flint).

    a. In verses 4–5, you can see the relationship that God the Son had with God the Father. Unlike the first Adam, who did not heed his Father's voice, this second Adam does. He models for us what it means to be a true disciple. What do you learn about Him in these verses?

    b. Describe the mind-set of Christ reflected in verses 6–7.

c. In the chapter, the author gave Jane Eyre as an example of standing firm despite the sacrifice demanded. Like Jesus, she was setting her face like flint. Where do you sense God asking you to stand firm, to set your face like flint today?

12. Read Isaiah 52:13–15. Why were people shocked at the appearance of Jesus on the cross?

*Today I spied God when . . .*

## Day Five: Isaiah 53, the Golden Chapter of the Old Testament

We are approaching holy ground, so imitate the attitude of Moses and take off your shoes (Exodus 3:5).

13. Read Isaiah 53:1–3.

a. What question is asked in verse 1?

b. What evidence supports the statement given in verses 2–3?

c. Why do you think people rejected Christ in His day? In our day?

14. Read verses 4–6 aloud, and then comment on whatever becomes radioactive to you and explain why.

15. Do the same with verses 7–9.

16. Do the same with verses 10–12.

17. Looking over Isaiah 52:13–53:12, find as many prophecies as you can that have been fulfilled.

18. Meditate on Isaiah 53:11: "Out of the anguish of his soul he shall see and be satisfied." What do you think Christ saw that satisfied Him? (Reading Isaiah 62:4–5 may help.) What does this mean to you?

19. What comfort have you found in this week's lessons?

*Today I spied God when . . .*


## Prayer Time

In small groups, begin with praise, using Isaiah 53. Then lift up your own request and allow others to support you.

# THIRTEEN

# Homesick No More

## *The Best Is Yet to Come*

> "I have come home at last! This is my real
> country! I belong here. This is the land I have
> been looking for all my life, though I never
> knew it till now. . . . Come further up, come
> further in!"
>
> —the UNICORN, in *The Last Battle*

Heaven once seemed daunting to me, otherworldly, and dare I say, boring? I didn't want to rest for eternity, nor did I want an eternal church service. When I read Revelation, I was not comforted. Streets of gold instead of forests of green? A celestial city instead of the sunny shore? I love the Wisconsin woods in which I'm blessed to live, with waves lapping on the shore and seagulls swooping through the sky. Revelation seemed to imply that the sunsets, starry nights, and seas I loved would all be gone. While I knew it would be wonderful to be with Jesus, the rest sounded cold—and honestly, a little scary.

I am eager to tell you how wrong I was! Isaiah is going to make us homesick for our real home. We can throw away our bucket list, for this earth is not our last chance at all. We don't have to sail the isles of Greece or see the penguins of Antarctica before we die—we'll have it all "at the renewal of all things" (Matthew 19:28, NIV). Understanding this has helped loosen my grasp on this world, for what I love on this earth will be in the world to come.

# The Renewal of All Things

Job, Isaiah, Jesus, Peter, and John all speak of the "renewal" or "restoration" of all things. N. T. Wright explains, "It is not we who go to heaven, it is heaven that comes to earth.... It is the final answer to the Lord's prayer, that God's kingdom will come and his will be done on earth as in heaven."[1] Our new life is *not* going to be in some ethereal place in the sky, but it will occur right here on this earth we love, only on an earth made new. Though this earth will burn and disappear, God will re-create it, making it unimaginably better, and join it to the new heaven, and we, His bride, the people of God, will live there in peace and joy forever.

> Behold, I create new heavens
> and a new earth,
> and the former things shall not be remembered
> or come into mind.
> But be glad and rejoice forever
> in that which I create.
> —Isaiah 65:17–18

This new heaven and new earth will be as tangible as the forests of Germany, the white sand beaches of Maui, and the animal-filled plains of Africa.

Most of us have a place we love on this earth, a place that feels the most like home, and the thought of never living there again seems sad. But wait! I love how Wendell Berry pictures this in his novels, which all take place in Port William, Kentucky, a fictional rural town nestled among wooded bluffs near a winding river. Berry writes that Port William "is eternal, always here and now, and going on forever," because "some day there will be a new heaven and a new earth and a new Port William coming down from heaven, adorned as a bride for her husband, and whoever has known her before will know her then."[2]

I like that thought, knowing that even if I don't see a new Ephraim, Wisconsin, in the new world, what I will see will be even better, will feel even more like home, and will absolutely "fit" me, for the One who knit me together in my mother's womb knows me better than I know myself and knows how to bring me unimaginable joy.

When I hear Phillip Phillips singing "Home," it so resonates with me, for I imagine Jesus singing it to me when I leave this world, urging me to hold on to Him as we go,

as we roll down this unfamiliar road . . .
'cause I'm going to make this place your home.[3]

Our world is beautiful but fallen, so we shall be so glad to have it "new-created" (Revelation 21:2, MSG). My corner of the world is so lovely that it attracts tourists by the millions, but like every vacation spot, it is also broken. Hurricane-force winds have wrapped my canoe around a tree, destroyed my pier, and brought cedars crashing down on my roof. Every May we have an Exodus-like plague of mayflies forcing us indoors when we are so ready to be out! Man has also brought trouble to this idyllic peninsula jutting into Lake Michigan. When man overharvested lake trout, he killed the natural predator of a slimy tiny fish called the alewife. Alewives began to populate beyond the point of survival. For a decade or more, before man could remedy his error, we'd look out at a sea of dead fish floating on our once beautiful lake. The waves would bring their carcasses in, piling up in huge mounds, staring out at us with accusing glassy eyes. The men on the shore would shovel them into wheelbarrows and bury them in the woods, but the stench persisted, permeating the once oh-so-fresh air.

But at the renewal of all things, the Great Lakes will be made clean and clear again and we will swim in them with our strong and glorified bodies. For just like us, the earth has been in bondage ever since the Fall and has been groaning, waiting for its redemption. Isaiah 55:12 tells us,

You shall go out in joy
    and be led forth in peace;
the mountains and the hills before you
    shall break forth into singing,
    and all the trees of the field shall clap their hands.

Jesus used the phrase "the renewal of all things," or, in Greek, the "*palingenesia,* which is derived from two root words: *paling,* meaning 'again,' and *genesia,* meaning 'beginning.'[4] We're going back to Eden but to an Eden restored. Jesus speaks of this almost casually:

> I tell you the truth, at the renewal of all things, when the Son of Man sits on his
> glorious throne. . . . everyone who has left houses or brothers or sisters or father
> or mother or children or fields for my sake will receive a hundred times
> as much and will inherit eternal life.
> —Matthew 19:28–29, NIV

At "the renewal of all things," not only will God give us back what was lost, but He will renew it to be a thousand times better. It took the Lord *six* days to make this beautiful earth, but it has been two thousand years since He told us He was going away to prepare a place for us. So can you even imagine what that place will look like? Paul, quoting Isaiah 64:4, says,

> As it is written,
> "What no eye has seen, nor ear heard,
>     nor the heart of man imagined,
> what God has prepared for those who love him."
> —1 Corinthians 2:9

Ecclesiastes says God "has put eternity into man's heart" (3:11). Blaise Pascal speaks of a time (Eden) when there was happiness in the human race, but "all that now remains is the outline and empty trace."[5] We are homesick! We live in a world under the curse and have long stretches of sorrow, sin, sickness, and strife. Yet in the midst of that sorrow, God gives us snatches of joy, echoes of Eden. I've tasted it when I was falling in love with Steve, when I held our newborn babies, when spring bursts forth in all her glory, and when a grandchild runs toward me with sparkling eyes and open arms. And oh, how I've tasted it in Christian fellowship: summer nights on the back porch, sharing our hearts and our Lord, all the while watching the setting sun spill violet across the waves.

But these fragile moments melt like snowflakes under the sun. I cannot hold on to them, and pursuing them so often fails, leaving me frustrated and sad, crying, "Vanity of vanities," like the writer of Ecclesiastes (1:2), chasing things under the sun.

I remember planning a picnic for our young family in Gas Works Park in Seattle. I imagined Steve flying kites with the boys while baby Sally delighted in the scene. Then we'd all relax on the grassy hill with the gourmet lunch I had carefully prepared, laughing and loving one another.

But as we were leaving for our glorious day, Steve got an emergency call at the hospital. I let him know how disappointed I was, and I could tell he felt bad. In a self-pitying mood, I took the children alone. The only kite that we got off the ground got caught in a tree, and the boys blamed each other, angry words flying. When I tried to put baby Sally on the grass, she held up her feet as if I were putting her on snakes, crying hysterically. The boys deemed the lunch gross. Then the sun disappeared and dark clouds began to pelt us with rain.

So often our dreams disappoint.

As C. S. Lewis says, "If I find in myself a desire which no experience in this world can satisfy, the most probable explanation is that I was made for another world."[6] We are longing for our "true country," the breathtaking land where we will be with Jesus and our loved ones, where we will laugh and love with new strong, healthy bodies like His resurrected body. We will never face cancer or painful goodbyes again. We will no longer be hurting one another through our sin but only bringing one another continual joy. Work will no longer be a curse but exciting and fulfilling. And the earth will be set free of biting flies, poison ivy, decay, and pollution. There will be clear rivers running through fields of wildflowers and green mansions of forests. Though we did not know it, it is for *this* land that we are homesick.

## A Vision of a World Made New

The reason I had such a skewed view of heaven was because I started with the climax in Revelation, where the mixed metaphors are rapidly reeling: After "Babylon the great, mother of prostitutes" (17:5) has been "thrown down with violence" (18:21), John sees another city, a "new Jerusalem," coming down out of heaven "prepared as a bride adorned for her husband" (21:2). We learn this bride is preparing for a marriage to a lamb who has been slain (19:7). This kaleidoscope of metaphors may not only make us feel dizzy but frightened, thinking heaven might be like something out of *Star Wars*.

But if we consider the threads of this story that have wound their way from Genesis on, we can get our bearings, and these wild metaphors make sense. So let's do a brief review to get ready for the prophets' vision of the world made new.

## A Tale of Two Cities

"The whole Bible," the Scottish preacher Eric Alexander says, "is in a very real sense a tale of two cities."[7] Babylon first appeared in Genesis 11 with the tower of Babel, and therefore it represents those attempting to make a name for themselves apart from God. The two peoples of Babylon and Jerusalem are descendants of Cain and Abel, representing the children of Satan and the children of God.

The children of Satan make up the city of Babylon that persecutes and enslaves the children of God, just as Cain persecuted Abel, and Ishmael persecuted Isaac. The captivity that God's people experienced in Babylon parallels the picture of the sorrow we experience as captives of Satan. Jesus, in Luke 4:18, quotes Isaiah and tells the astonished listeners that He is the one whom God has anointed to set the captives free. We were captive, but we *have* been set free from the penalty of sin, *are* being set free from the power of sin, and one day *will* be set free from the presence of sin when "Babylon the great" is cast down forever:

> Fallen, fallen is Babylon the great!
> She has become a dwelling place for demons.
> —Revelation 18:2

## The Unblemished Lamb

The story of the Lamb threads throughout Scripture, with every slain lamb pointing to Jesus, who was, Isaiah 53:7 tells us, "like a lamb that is led to the slaughter." The good news of Christianity, as opposed to every other religion, is that our entrance into this new heaven and new earth depends not on our righteousness but on the righteousness of the Lamb without blemish or spot. Our trust in Him clothes us in a pure wedding garment, and we are welcomed into the world He has made new.

## The Bride and the Bridegroom

The story of the bride also runs from Genesis to Revelation. The Bible begins with a wedding, ends with a wedding, and is shot through with pictures of a faithful Bridegroom rescuing, loving, and transforming an unfaithful bride. And now in Isaiah we begin to understand the beautiful truth that caused Jesus to go through the anguish that He did. He set His face like flint to rescue, redeem, and restore us so that we could live forever with Him in a new heaven and a new earth. Isaiah says of true believers who make up the bride,

> You shall no more be termed Forsaken,
>     and your land shall no more be termed Desolate,
> but you shall be called My Delight Is in Her. . . .
> And as the bridegroom rejoices over the bride,
>     so shall your God rejoice over you.
>     —62:4–5

Jesus will delight in us and we in Him, and our land will be like the most glorious spring you can imagine. In a sense, every spring we get a preview of the "renewal of all things." In northern Wisconsin we wait with longing for spring, for she is always late. We grumble in May when there is yet another snowstorm. But oh! When she arrives, she is like a beautiful woman late for a date—she is *so* glorious that all is forgiven. Blue forget-me-nots blanket the forest, the fragrance of lilacs fills the air, the cherry orchards dance with blossoms in the breeze, the trees burst with spring green, and the seagulls soar, once again dipping in a lake shimmering in the sun.

This is the world delightfully pictured in the Song of Songs, which is, indeed, a picture of the curse reversed and Eden restored. Jesus will call the names of everyone written in the book of life, and we *will* rise from the dead with our new glorious bodies, heeding the call spoken by the bridegroom in the Song of Songs:

> Arise, my love, my beautiful one,
>     and come away,
> for behold, the winter is past;
>     the rain is over and gone.
> The flowers appear on the earth,
>     the time of singing has come,
> and the voice of the turtledove
>     is heard in our land.
>     —2:10–12

## Everything Sad Will Be Untrue

We also see in Isaiah's words that we will not lose anything good in this life! I think that is what J. R. R. Tolkien meant when his character Sam Gamgee says, "Is everything sad going to come untrue?"[8] It isn't just that the glory will *compensate* for the sorrow but that somehow the suffering we experienced here on earth will make the glory *better*. I don't know how, but that is the mystery to which prophet after prophet alludes.

Our bodies, though they may have been racked with arthritis, cancer, or just wrinkles and fat, will be made new! Our bodies will be like Jesus's glorious resurrection body, and they will never decay or grow old again.

Isaiah uses pictures we understand to help us glimpse this new reality. He says,

No more shall there be in it
an infant who lives but a few days,
or an old man who does not fill out his days.
—65:20

This does not mean that there will be death in the new earth, for we are clearly told in Revelation that there will be no more death. This means, instead, that we will never again have the sorrow of burying an infant or a man whose life was cut short. And our lives will be so glorious, that, Isaiah says, "the former things shall not be remembered or come into mind" (verse 17).

I still have nightmares about the last painful days Steve had on earth, but when I see him at "the renewal of all things" and he has his new healthy, young, glorious resurrection body, all those sad memories will be erased forever.

Parents will hold their babies lost through genocide, miscarriage, or abortion. How old will they be? I don't know—but Isaiah gives us a picture of the joys of some kind of family life, of building homes and not being uprooted, of working and loving together and enjoying the fruits of our labors:

They shall build houses and inhabit them;
they shall plant vineyards and eat their fruit.
They shall not build and another inhabit;
they shall not plant and another eat;

for like the days of a tree shall the days of my people be.

—verses 21–22

After Steve died, I was having dinner with a friend who has been single all her life. When I told her how eager my children and I were to be with Steve again in the new earth, she became very quiet. Finally, she explained that it had been hard for her to be single and childless on earth, and now I was telling her that sorrow was going to continue eternally? I would walk off happily ever after with Steve and our children and she would still be alone?

No! That will not be the scenario! Though I see "through a glass, darkly," Isaiah gives us this picture of family life for everyone:

"Sing, O barren one, who did not bear;
     break forth into singing and cry aloud,
     you who have not been in labor!
For the children of the desolate one will be more
     than the children of her who is married," says the LORD.

—54:1

We are all going to have family. My friend has ministered to millions with her music, and God has used her gifts to bring so many to Christ. She will definitely, as Isaiah says, have to "enlarge [her] tent" (verse 2), for she will have *so* many spiritual children. And as the extroverted Italian that she is, she loves parties, so I picture lanterns in the trees, a brook rippling through the garden, tables set with flowers, a meal and wine better than that of the best Italian restaurant, and her laughing and enjoying her children in the family of God. All the while Jesus is present and delighting in what He has given her.

Indeed, no matter our marital state on earth, single or married, happily or unhappily, we will *all* know love like we've never tasted before. God will be rejoicing in us, and we in Him, and all of us in one another.

## The Animal Kingdom

How often the question is raised, Will we have our pets in heaven? I don't know that either, but I do know there will be animals there. And, as Isaiah 65:25 tells us, never will my dog quarrel with the porcupine or skunk again, for all those at enmity will be at peace:

> The wolf and the lamb shall graze together,
>      the lion shall eat straw like the ox.

Lewis's picture of the children riding on Aslan the Lion, frolicking in the meadow, may actually become a reality! We will be able to play and delight in all the animals, for,

> "They shall not hurt or destroy
>      in all my holy mountain,"
> says the LORD.

God is a Redeemer! He will redeem all that He pronounced "good" in Genesis and make it even better.

## Enjoying the Work of Our Hands

Though I love a good night's sleep, I don't want to rest eternally, which is what some funerals make me think is in store. But no! We will, as on earth, still be working, not with toil and frustration but with joy!

> My chosen shall long enjoy the work of their hands.
>      —Isaiah 65:22

So many people hate their work, but it was not that way before the Fall—and it won't be that way in the new-created world.

Soon after Steve died, my son JR had a dream of his father, in which Steve came to visit him. JR said, "He looked *so* good. He couldn't stay long, but he told me he loved me and would see me soon. He said he had a lot of wonderful work to do—not medicine though, of course, for there were no sick people where he was. And then he laughed his great laugh and disappeared."

I am so blessed to have enjoyed writing for most of my adult life, yet there are frustrating times when nothing seems to work or I throw away a whole year's worth of effort. I've also written things that embarrassed me later.

After I was widowed, I read what I had written twenty years earlier about the newly widowed Naomi. I'd said she was too dependent on her husband. I thought, *How lacking in empathy! You had ice water running through your veins.* Thankfully, I was blessed with a publisher who was willing to change it in the next printing.

But that is not how work will ever be in the new Eden, for before I even call out to God, Isaiah tells me that He will answer (verse 24), helping me write not only beautifully but only what is kind and true. And perhaps I will be able to take classes from C. S. Lewis, Blaise Pascal, John Donne, and my favorite psalmist, Asaph!

The frustrations of *every* kind of work will be gone—even the frustrations and sorrows of parenting where we see children become rebellious or face heartache.

> They shall not labor in vain
> or bear children for calamity,
> for they shall be the offspring of the blessed of the LORD,
> and their descendants with them.
> —verse 23

Some of my greatest sorrows have come when I have watched a child suffer enormous wounds from this sinful world. In this world we live in today, we cannot even send our children off to school without fearing a mass shooting. But that will not be true "at the renewal of all things." As J. Alec Motyer writes, "There is no darker cloud over a parent's life than to see tragedy touch a beloved child on whom love and hope is set. Such will never be the case in the new Jerusalem, for 'they will be a seed blessed by the Lord.'"[9]

We are *all* homesick for heaven. We all have a sense that this earth is not how things are meant to be.

## The New Jerusalem

I love how all these pictures come together in Scripture, like puzzle pieces that finally fit. When I looked at this puzzle piece from Revelation 21:2 all by itself, I was confused: "I saw the holy city, new Jerusalem, coming down out of heaven from God, prepared as a bride adorned for her husband."

What is it? A city? A woman?

But now I understand. The New Jerusalem is the "new-created" Old Jerusalem, where God's people are no longer estranged from Him but are rejoicing, "You are my God!" and He is saying, "And you are my people!" Look at Isaiah 65:18–19:

> Be glad and rejoice forever
>     in that which I create;
> for behold, I create Jerusalem to be a joy,
>     and her people to be a gladness.
> I will rejoice in Jerusalem
>     and be glad in my people;
> no more shall be heard in it the sound of weeping
>     and the cry of distress.

You may remember how God commanded Hosea to marry an unfaithful woman as a living mural of the heartbreak Israel was bringing to God. Hosea's wife has illegitimate children through her lovers, and one is named Not My People! But it is a temporary situation, for hearts will be changed, and one day, Hosea prophesies, God "will say to Not My People, 'You are my people'; and he shall say, 'You are my God'" (Hosea 2:23). It is still a mystery to me how and when all this will happen, but indeed we know that God has His ways of transforming the hardest hearts, for He is looking forward to the New Jerusalem, when He will rejoice in His bride and she in Him.

This also sheds light on the mysterious book of the Song of Songs, for indeed, though this is an earthly human love story, it points to the mysterious love story of Christ for His bride. When the bride in the Song rejoices, "I am my beloved's and my beloved is mine" (6:3), we hear the echo of "You are my God and I am your people." The whole Bible is a love story, and the New Jerusalem, indeed, is a bride, and the dwelling place of God and His people rejoice in one another like newlyweds. So now the scene in Revelation of the New Jerusalem coming down dressed as a bride for her husband does not seem so strange at all.

## "Come, Everyone Who Thirsts"

Not everyone will be in the new heaven and new earth, although many funerals lead you to believe otherwise. As in the parable of the wedding banquet that Jesus tells, some will try to get in without a wedding garment, without the cleansing that can come only through repentance and faith in the shed blood of Christ.

Let's see how the scene unfolds.

> "Friend, how did you get in here without a wedding garment?" And he was speechless. Then the king said to the attendants, "Bind him hand and foot and cast him into the outer darkness. In that place there will be weeping and gnashing of teeth."
> — Matthew 22:12–13

But indeed, the invitation to our real home *is* open to all who choose to receive the free gift Jesus offers. He paid the price He did not owe so that we could have the life we do not deserve. It is a free gift, but you must come to Him in repentance and faith. Isaiah puts it like this:

> Come, everyone who thirsts,
>     come to the waters;
> and he who has no money,
>     come, buy and eat!
> Come, buy wine and milk
>     without money and without price.
>     —Isaiah 55:1

This is the good news of the gospel. This is the thread, the rescue, that winds its way through *all* of the Scriptures. The same promise of a free rescue that we saw in all the Scriptures—including the books of Moses, the Psalms, and in the prophet Isaiah—comes full circle at the close of Revelation: "The Spirit and the Bride say, 'Come.' And let the one who hears say, 'Come.' And let the one who is thirsty come; let the one who desires take the water of life without price" (22:17).

My hope is that seeing this same story from Genesis to Revelation will give you great confidence in the reliability of the Scriptures and the truths they hold. For the Jesus who surprised the two on the road to Emmaus, and surprises us in our everyday lives, is not at all finished surprising us.

## Bible Study Thirteen

As a group, view the related video and share comments: go to deebrestin.com and click on *The Jesus Who Surprises* under Free Teaching Videos. Also, as an option for going deeper, listen online to "Isaiah 65" by Eric Alexander. And a perfect closing for this study is the video "Is He Worthy?" by Andrew Peterson.

### Week Thirteen God Hunt

Jerram Barrs, professor at Covenant Seminary, uses the phrase *echoes of Eden,* meaning something you see, hear, or experience that reminds you of what the world was like before it all went wrong. You may come upon it in the arts, nature, or even the kindness of strangers. Be alert and list any echoes of Eden in your God Hunts this week.

### Day One: Chapter Review

1. Read and highlight the chapter. What are two thoughts that impressed you?

2. If you listened to Eric Alexander, please share your comments here.

   *Today I spied God when . . .*

### Day Two: A Tale of Two Cities

Revelation can seem quite strange if you start there, so let's instead review the threads, beginning with a tale of two cities: Babylon and Jerusalem.

3. Read Genesis 11:1–9 and explain *why* the people made a tower. What lie were they believing?

4. Review Psalm 137 and describe the pain of God's people as captives in Babylon.

5. What pain have you experienced because of bondage to sin and to Satan? If you are being delivered in certain areas, share that, too.

6. Read Revelation 18:2. What understanding do you now have of this verse?

7. Read Revelation 21:1–4. What understanding do you now have of this passage?

*Today I spied God when . . .*

## Day Three: The Lamb and the Bride and Bridegroom

8. Review Genesis 22:7–8. What question does Isaac ask, and how does Abraham answer? What does this story foreshadow?

9. Read Isaiah 53:4–7. How was Jesus to be like a lamb?

10. Read Revelation 19:6–8 and explain this passage in light of what you've learned about the Lamb.

11. What was Adam's reaction when God brought Eve to him in Genesis 2:23? What comparison does Isaiah 62:3–5 make?

12. What common thread can you trace through the following passages? Also, share any way this impacts you.

a. Song of Songs 6:3

b. Hosea 2:23

c. Isaiah 65:17–19

d. Revelation 21:1–4

*Today I spied God when . . .*

## Day Four: All Things New (Part 1)

To prepare your heart for today, watch the YouTube video called "Is He Worthy?" by Andrew Peterson.

13. What do you remember from the chapter about the following:

   a. What does the Greek word *palingenesia* mean?

   b. How is spring a mini preview of the palingenesia?

   c. What does C. S. Lewis say we should learn when our dreams in this world disappoint?

   d. Why don't we need a bucket list? (Or do you think we do? If so, why?)

14. Read Matthew 19:28–29. How does Jesus speak of the palingenesia, and what do you learn from His words?

15. Read Isaiah 65:17–20 aloud and share any meditations on it.

16. Read Isaiah 65:17–20 again.

a. What stands out to you and why?

b. What do you think God means by verse 20? How literally do you think we should take His words and why?

c. How might you use the truths here to speak to your soul when you are anxious or in grief?

17. Read verses 21–22 aloud and share any meditations on them.

18. Read Isaiah 65:21–22 again.

a. What in the palingensia will be different from this world today?

b. Is this picture of heaven different from what you pictured in the past? If so, explain.

*Today I spied God when . . .*

## Day Five: All Things New (Part 2)

19. Read Isaiah 54:1–8 and share your meditations. Also share how this passage could be a comfort to those deprived of marriage or parenting in this life.

20. Read Isaiah 65:23–25 and share your meditations.

21. Read Isaiah 65:23–25 again.

    a. What promise do you find in verse 23, and what might this mean to you or someone you love who has lost children or seen them suffer?

    b. What do you think verse 24 tells us about the new heaven and new earth?

    c. What do you learn about animals in the palingenesia?

    d. What does "dust shall be the serpent's food" refer to, do you think?

22. In a few sentences, how would you describe heaven to another person, based on Scripture?

23. Review:

    a. Share two things you want to remember from part 1: "How the Story Began: The Books of Moses."

    b. Share two things you want to remember from part 2: "How to Live in the Story: The Psalms."

    c. Share two things you want to remember from part 3: "How the Story Will End: The Prophets."

24. How has Jesus surprised you through this book and Bible study? How have you been changed?

*Today I spied God when . . .*

## Prayer Time

Begin with thanksgiving for promises you have discovered or truths you have learned over the past few weeks. Then take time to bless one another with eyes open and looking at one another. The facilitator will lift up each person, and then a few others will share a blessing or affirmation over that individual. Then go to the next.

# Facilitator Resources

# Hints for Group Facilitators

## *Inviting Others to This Study*

In an email inviting people to this study, link to a promotional video for this book, available on Amazon and at the Dee Brestin Ministries website.

## *Optional Teaching Videos*

Excellent short videos—under fifteen minutes for each chapter—feature teaching from Dee and testimonies from women who did this study. These are also found at Dee's website and on DVDs online. You can show these before each discussion (preferable) or assign them as part of the homework by linking to the applicable web page.

## *The Role of a Facilitator*

A facilitator is not a teacher but a tool of the Holy Spirit to help group members discover truths together by looking into the Word and sharing what God is showing them. Here are some ideas to help you in this important role:

- Place the chairs in as small a circle as possible, because space inhibits sharing.
- Homework is important, so set the standard high. Pray for members during the week, and expect homework to be done between each group gathering.
- If some members in the group were not able to get their book ahead of time, do the get-acquainted lesson at the first meeting.
- Begin each week by showing the short introductory video (if you are opting to use the videos).
- Begin the discussion by going around the circle and asking members to share, briefly, their very best God Hunt of the week. This is a great

icebreaker, and icebreakers really do help a group warm up and get comfortable. Skipping them is a mistake!

- There is great value in reading the scriptural text aloud and allowing time for comments before you dive into the questions.
- Each week's study has more questions than you will have time to answer together. Circle ahead of time the questions that lead to more discussion and assume that members have answered the fact-gathering questions on their own.
- Always ask both of the questions under Day One—one is about the chapter and the other about the optional sermon. Also, the final question for each week's study is important.
- If a discussion takes off, let it go unless it really gets off topic. That's moving with the Spirit.
- Encourage people with a nod, smile, or word or two when they share. If an answer is significantly off track, pray that someone else will question it, which will be perceived as less threatening than your questioning it. You might say, "That's interesting—I have never heard that before. What does someone else think?" You can also direct the group back to the text. Your goal is to provide a safe, nonthreatening time of discussion so people will keep coming back and the Spirit and the Word will lead them into truth.
- If someone in the group tends to dominate the discussion, here are some things that can help:
  - Say something like, "Shy people need pauses to gather courage to speak up, so if you are one who talks easily, hold back to help others. Share a few times, but don't jump in every time there is a silence."
  - Go around the circle with some questions so everyone has a chance to answer. Often the opening questions or closing ones are good for this.
  - Ask, "Can we hear from someone who hasn't had a chance to share?'
  - If it continues to be a problem, take the individual aside privately and ask for his or her help, repeating what you said about shy people.
  - After the first study, send an email, text, or note to the people who came, thanking them for coming and affirming them in some small way. The main reason people drop out of groups is because they don't feel valued.

# Lesson-by-Lesson Facilitator Notes

Answers to questions can be found in the Bible text or in the chapter text. In this section, you'll find help for some of the more challenging questions, which are marked in each lesson with an asterisk (*).

## Optional Get-Acquainted Bible Study

If you finish early, feel free to get started together on Day Two of Bible Study One, first reading aloud Luke 24:1–12.

## Bible Study One

At the start of Day Two, be sure to have someone read aloud the main text (Luke 24:1–12) and take time for comments. Don't be afraid of silences; they give the shy members time to speak up. Do the same when you get to verses 13–35 on Day Three and verses 36–46 on Day Five.

12a. We don't know if the two on the road were in the upper room at the Last Supper, when Jesus broke the bread and said, "This is My body," but they probably had heard about it from the others.

13. This would be a great question to hear from many about. If your group is small, you could go around the circle, giving individuals the freedom to say, "Pass."

15. All of the Old Testament can be divided into three types of literature, or genres: history (Genesis through Esther), poetry (Job through the Song of Songs), and prophecy (Isaiah through Malachi). Jesus mentioned each when he said, "The Law of Moses and the Prophets and the Psalms must be fulfilled" (Luke 24:44). These represent all three parts of the Old Testament.

17. Hear from many on this question.

Prayer Time: Many people are uncomfortable praying aloud in groups, so this is a way to ease them into it, just having them share one takeaway or God Hunt for which they are thankful. Tell them they can keep their eyes open—it still "counts" as prayer! Their words can be as simple as "Thank you for this group." Or they can say, "Pass."

## Bible Study Two

Remember to begin with members sharing their best God Hunt answer of the week and their responses to both of the questions from Day One. Remember also to read aloud key passages throughout the study and get comments, allowing time for silence between answers.

14. Because God is relational, we are too. We long to be in relationship.

Because both male and female are in the image of God, the image of

God is not reflected completely by just one gender; both are necessary.

18/19. These closing questions are important to ask.

Prayer Time: Tell the group you will be breaking into smaller groups to pray. In the smaller groups, each person should share a personal need rather than for her uncle Tom's neighbor. A prayer request could be as simple as "Help me complete the homework" or "I need wisdom with my strong-willed toddler."

If several participants are new to group prayer, you could model this for the whole group with two people who are comfortable with prayer. (Practice with them ahead of time.) Explain that you are demonstrating what the prayer would look like after you have gone around and asked for a personal prayer request from everyone. Now you lift up their names. This is sometimes called "popcorn prayer" because people share briefly (pop) and when the popping stops, you move to the next person. For example:

**You:** Let's pray for Molly.

**Tom:** Thank you that Molly experienced your help with her house decisions.

**You:** Please help Molly to have wisdom in her finances.

**Molly:** Yes, Lord!

*(The popping prayers pause, so you move on to the next person.)*

**You:** Let's pray for Tom.

**Molly:** Thank you that Tom had a good conversation with his father.

**Lynn:** Please continue to move in that relationship.

*(The popping prayers pause, so you move on to the next person.)*

## Bible Study Three

Begin with the best God Hunt discoveries of the week and the opening two questions.

3a. The lie is always some form of God not having our best interests at heart; therefore, the temptation is to go our own way.

3c. Though it is usually good for the facilitator not to be the first to answer, when the question calls for vulnerability, you should be prepared to model that if no one else jumps in.

7b. Jesus, for He is the only one who did not have a human father, therefore, "the offspring of a woman."

8. To be just, sin must be punished—and it was, when Christ died in our stead. To be loving, Christ had to be willing to take the burden of our sins on Himself, and He was.

9c. Instead of each endeavoring to control the other, endeavor to be in submission to each other, putting your spouse's needs ahead of your own and dying to self. As the facilitator, be sure to ask for illustrations for this one.

## Bible Study Four

Begin with the best God Hunt encounters of the week and the opening two questions.

10c. If we put God first, we will relinquish control to Him rather than going our own way and breaking His commandments.

11. This answer is similar to that of 10c. Idolatry is the sin beneath the sin, so if we aren't walking in the light, in love, or in truth, a heart idol is at work.

12. Many struggle with the black-and-white statements of 1 John, but we know because of 1:8 ("If we say we have no sin, we deceive ourselves") that John isn't saying a child of God doesn't sin but that the persistent direction of his or her life is to honor God. By contrast, the persistent direction of a child of Satan is to not care about honoring God. It has to do with which "seed" is in you.

13b. Control seems most likely; instead of doing it God's way (repenting of his heart attitude), Cain takes the reins and solves the problem his way, through murder.

## Bible Study Five

5. Eliphaz would have fallen on the religious side of the chart. He advises Job in 4:6 to trust in Job's own piety, his own righteousness. And his rhetorical question in verse 7 implies that bad things don't happen to good people, but that is not what Scripture or life tells us. All the disciples except John were martyred, and so has it been with many of the godliest people who ever lived.

In verses 12–16, we actually see an evil, lying spirit inspiring Eliphaz. As Mike Mason notes, "One even gets the feeling that, as frightening as this experience was, Eliphaz would not have missed it for anything."[1]

11. Religious: sinful, slaves, does not love Christ. Gospel: abides, set free, loves Christ.

15d. You can direct group members to the Tim Keller chart for help if needed. Then rephrase the question with an example: "How does religion enslave and lead to barrenness, and how does the gospel set free and lead to fruitfulness? For example, when criticized, if you can't stop thinking about it, it enslaves and hurts you. But if, because of the gospel, you are confident of your worth, you can listen receptively to criticism and respond to it, and that leads to freedom and fruitfulness."

## Bible Study Six

The sacrifice of Isaac is a challenging story, so you will find it helpful to listen to Tim Keller's sermon to prepare for facilitating this lesson.

## Bible Study Seven

Remember to keep asking for everyone's best God Hunt discovery of the week as an icebreaker!

8. This is a little challenging because Job asks a question (Job 14:14), then listens, and then reveals what God has put in his heart. One day, just as Jesus called the name of Lazarus, He will call Job's name and the name of every believer, and we will rise from the dead, each of us with a new body,

like Christ's resurrected body. He will do this because our transgressions have been covered over!

## Bible Study Eight

3c. Ezekiel sheds light on what otherwise is a confusing passage, for many have thought the water Jesus mentions in John 3:5 ("born of water and the Spirit") refers to water baptism or the water of the first birth. But the parallel with Ezekiel shows us that this new birth comes not through man but through God. God cleanses us as He leads us to repentance, and then He puts His Spirit within us.

Prayer Time: You might comment that so often our prayers are for God to change circumstances but that we should also be continually asking Him to change our hearts, to give us the power to overcome our idols and the faith to trust His love.

## Bible Study Nine

5f. Waves and breakers can represent troubles that keep coming, yet we also see from the second part of Psalm 42:7 that they can represent the steadfast love and songs of the Lord. It's significant that the psalmist refers to "all your breakers and your waves."

5g. The psalmist is in distress, yet just as Jonah knows God cast him into the sea (Jonah 2:3) and says, "I am driven away from your sight," he also knows he "shall again look upon [the LORD's] holy temple" (verse 4).

Encourage everyone to watch both Michael Reeves's twenty-minute video and Lucy's five-minute testimony before next week, as these will shed great light on a difficult study.

## Bible Study Ten

4. We know Scripture is inspired by God and inerrant—and yet not dictated. This verse seems to imply that God fills the hearts of the writers so that His thoughts overflow, but amazingly, He still uses the personalities and temperaments of the people He created and called.

11c. Our Bridegroom, Jesus, died that we might live. He also asks us to die to ourselves, putting Him before other loves, even our family (Psalm 45:10). But with every death there is a resurrection!

## Bible Study Eleven

If you choose to divide this study into two meetings, assign the first three days for the first week and go as far as you can in discussion. Then assign the rest. If you are going to do it all in one week, circle a few questions from each day and be sure to do Day Five.

3c. Jesus stops before reading "and the day of vengeance of our God" (Isaiah 61:2) because in His first coming, He came to bear vengeance rather than bring it. This is what He wants to emphasize, but He will later speak of the final judgment, when judgment will come.

7. You may need to go first to model vulnerability.

8. The gospel teaches our hearts to fear (for we are made aware of our sin, as Isaiah is) and also relieves our fear (after the hot coal touches his lips, Isaiah feels purified).

13b. You could rephrase this, asking them to finish this sentence with an illustration: "How do people, even children, refer to this unwritten moral law when they say, 'It's not fair that you . . . '?"

## Bible Study Twelve

10b. The word *engraved* indicates sharp metal inflicting the words, leaving wounds. (See also John 20:27–28.) Jesus came to rescue His bride, and His crucifixion accomplished that.

## Bible Study Thirteen

If it is possible to plan a longer time today with a lunch or supper celebration, please do! This week's study is long, and the sharing should be rich and unhurried if possible. A meal also lends itself to a time of closure and reflection as you conclude your time together.

# Acknowledgments

### My Gifted Editor, Elisa Fryling Stanford

For the decades we have worked together, for the passion and gifting you bring, for our precious friendship, I continually thank God. You see what I cannot see, gently speaking the truth to me so that it can be clearer and stronger! Then I sit back and revel at the beauty He brings through putting our giftings together. I'm doubly thankful this time, for I know working on *The Jesus Who Surprises* was a step of faith for you, as you are in the midst of such a long and severe storm with Eden's illness. How I pray He will soon surprise us again with His joy!

### The Team at Multnomah

I am overjoyed to work with you again, a publisher whose foremost desire is to bring glory to God. I am so thankful for that heart motivation! Laura Barker is a wise visionary who listens, prays, and responds. Beverly Rykerd and Ginia Hairston Croker and their publicity and marketing teams are truly *the best*. They have been immensely creative, caring, and invested. The cover design by Kelly Howard is striking. Laura Wright is diligent and exact, making sure quotes are perfect, references correct, and questions clear. One of the ways we spy Jesus in our God Hunts in *The Jesus Who Surprises* is by seeing how He helps us to do our work in this world. I certainly spy Him through the team at Multnomah!

### The Video Team

How thankful I am for the *amazing* women from First Hope in Columbus, Georgia. I certainly had no idea how God would turn my giving a retreat for you into something much bigger for His kingdom! From the moment I met Suzanne McCluskey by phone, I sensed a kindred spirit. And then I met Mary Pat Beckum and the women of First Hope and was so impressed at their depth, the kind of depth you are more likely to see in less privileged countries. They had been discipled well! When it became evident that God was leading us together to do this video, I was thrilled, knowing that these women would have powerful testimonies about the ways Jesus surprised them! Justin Konsler,

First Hope's very gifted tech man, has a heart to glorify God by giving his time and talent. I also want to thank the W. C. Bradley Co. real-estate powerhouse for allowing us to film in its beautiful rooms and surroundings.

When I was praying about who to ask to do the edit, I thought of the wonderful videos Tim Mahoney had done for my book *Idol Lies* and dared to see if he would be willing to do the whole edit for *The Jesus Who Surprises*. To my great delight, he was, giving generously of his time and talent and working alongside the team of First Hope.

## Pilot Group

What a joy it was to test this study with women in many stages of spiritual growth in Door County, Wisconsin. I don't think I'll ever forget the joy we found together in "spying Jesus" every day and all through the Bible. You helped me know what was clear and what needed to be rephrased. Your joy in the study fueled my passion to make this as strong a study as I could. What fun we had on our God Hunts—and I'll never forget the excitement of many of you in discovering that the Bible is one great story! Your joy gave me such joy!

## My Family

This book is one of the most personal I've ever written, with intimate stories that involve all five of my children: James (JR), John, Sally, Beth, and Annie. Thank you for your graciousness! Your dad and I made many mistakes in raising you, so the glory truly goes to God that you are the men and women of God you are. Such joy God has given me in each of you, your spouses, and your precious children.

## Tim Keller, Mike Reeves, R. C. Sproul, and Eric Alexander

I'm so thankful for your free sermons available online so that those who are hungry for more of God can go deeper and so that your clear and passionate expositions can illuminate their understanding of the Jesus who surprises.

# Notes

## Optional Get-Acquainted Bible Study

1. Karen Mains gave our family the idea for the God Hunt in her book *The God Hunt: The Delightful Chase and the Wonder of Being Found* (Downers Grove, IL: InterVarsity, 2003).

## Chapter 1: A Journey of Surprises

1. Dr. Jeff Johnson, conversation with the author, summer of 2017.
2. Outline of Rudolf Otto's concept of the numinous, based on *The Idea of the Holy*, 2nd ed., trans. John W. Harvey (London: Oxford University Press, 1923), https://www2.kenyon.edu/Depts/Religion/Fac/Adler/Reln101/Otto.htm.
3. Darrell Bock, *Luke,* Baker Exegetical Commentary on the New Testament (Grand Rapids, MI: Baker, 1996), 1917.
4. John Piper, "Letter to an Incomplete, Insecure Teenager," Desiring God, July 16, 2011, www.desiringgod.org/articles/letter-to-an-incomplete-insecure-teenager.
5. Sally Lloyd-Jones, *The Jesus Storybook Bible: Every Story Whispers His Name* (Grand Rapids, MI: Zondervan, 2007), 17.

## Chapter 2: The God of the Dance

The epigraph is taken from John Piippo, "Bono's Conversion," July 27, 2012, www.johnpiippo.com/2012/07/bonos-conversion.html.

1. C. S. Lewis, *Surprised by Joy: The Shape of My Early Life* (San Francisco: HarperOne, 2017), 279–80.
2. John Wesley, "I Felt My Heart Strangely Warmed," *Journal of John Wesley,* Christian Classics Ethereal Library, www.ccel.org/ccel/wesley/journal.vi.ii.xvi.html.
3. "BreakPoint: Chuck Colson's Conversion," BreakPoint, October 16, 2017, www.breakpoint.org/2017/10/breakpoint-chuck-colsons-conversion.
4. Anne Lamott, *Traveling Mercies: Some Thoughts on Faith* (New York: Anchor, 1999), 48.
5. Linda Strom, *Karla Faye Tucker Set Free: Life and Faith on Death Row* (Colorado Springs, CO: WaterBrook, 2000), video 8 of *Idol Lies:* https://deebrestin.com/idol-lies.

6. Discipleship Unlimited, 2018. This number is based on statistics of women who have been through DU's eighteen-month program and remained out of prison for at least five years.

7. Michael Reeves, *Delighting in the Trinity: An Introduction to the Christian Faith* (Downers Grove, IL: InterVarsity, 2012), 40.

8. Richard Sibbes, "The Successful Seeker," in *Works of Richard Sibbes* (Edinburgh, UK: James Nichol, 1862–64), 6:113.

9. Brennan Manning, *Abba's Child: The Cry of the Heart for Intimate Belonging* (Colorado Springs, CO: NavPress, 1994), 128.

10. "Prayer Tips: George Müller," The Prayer Foundation, http://prayerfoundation .org/prayer_tips_george_mueller.htm.

11. Wallace Stegner, *Crossing to Safety* (New York: Modern Classics, 2002), 21.

12. Stegner, *Crossing to Safety,* 23.

13. John of the Cross, *The Collected Works of St. John of the Cross,* trans. Kieran Kavanaugh and Otilio Rodriguez, rev. ed. (Washington, DC: ICS Publications, 2010), 484.

14. Joni Eareckson Tada and Steven Estes, *When God Weeps: Why Our Sufferings Matter to the Almighty* (Grand Rapids, MI: Zondervan, 2000), 56.

## Chapter 3: He Showed Up with a Whip

The epigraph is taken from Timothy Keller, "Paradise Promised," Gospel in Life, November 12, 2000, MP3 audio, 36:21, https://gospelinlife.com/download s/paradise-promised-5209.

1. Abraham Lincoln, "Proclamation Appointing a National Fast Day," Abraham Lincoln Online, March 30, 1863, www.abrahamlincolnonline.org/lincoln /speeches/fast.htm.

2. Timothy J. Keller, "Nakedness and the Holiness of God," Gospel in Life, March 21, 1993, MP3 audio, 47:56, https://gospelinlife.com/downloads/nakedness -the-holiness-of-god-6247.

3. Mark Regnerus, "Christians Are Part of the Same Dating Pool as Everybody Else. That's Bad for the Church," *Washington Post,* September 5, 2017, www .washingtonpost.com/news/acts-of-faith/wp/2017/09/05/christians-are-part -of-the-same-dating-pool-as-everyone-else-thats-bad-for-the-church/?utm_term =.57350cfdd764.

4. Regnerus, "Christians Are Part of the Same Dating Pool."

5. Derek Kidner, *Genesis,* Tyndale Old Testament Commentaries (Downers Grove, IL: InterVarsity, 1981), 71.

## Chapter 4: Crouching Tiger, Hidden Dragon

1. Philip Yancey, *The Jesus I Never Knew* (Grand Rapids, MI: Zondervan, 2008), 268.
2. Josh Huynh, "Bob Newhart-Stop It," YouTube video, 6:20, September 1, 2010, www.youtube.com/watch?v=Ow0lr63y4Mw.
3. Lee Ezell, *The Missing Piece* (New York: Bantam, 1988).
4. Wesley Hill, *Washed and Waiting: Reflections on Christian Faithfulness and Homosexuality* (Grand Rapids, MI: Zondervan, 2010), 29.
5. Timothy Keller, *Encounters with Jesus: Unexpected Answers to Life's Biggest Questions* (New York: Penguin, 2015), 163.

## Chapter 5: Religion Versus the Gospel

The epigraph is taken from John Stott, *The Message of Galatians* (Downers Grove, IL: InterVarsity, 1984), 126.

1. Taken from Timothy Keller, *Gospel in Life Study Guide: Grace Changes Everything* (Grand Rapids, MI: Zondervan, 2010), 16, copyright © 2010 by Timothy Keller. Used by permission of Zondervan, www.zondervan.com.
2. Stott, *Message of Galatians,* 124.
3. D. Martyn Lloyd-Jones, *Spiritual Depression: Its Causes and Cures* (Grand Rapids: Eerdmans, 1965), 33–35.
4. Stott, *Message of Galatians,* 126.
5. Quoted in Keller, *Gospel in Life,* 18.
6. Stott, *Message of Galatians,* 127.

## Chapter 6: The Plotline of the Bible

1. Madeleine L'Engle, *Walking on Water: Reflections on Faith and Art* (New York: Convergent, 1980), 174.
2. L'Engle, *Walking on Water,* 175.
3. L'Engle, *Walking on Water,* 177.
4. C. S. Lewis, *The Lion, the Witch and the Wardrobe* (Glasgow: William Collins and Sons, 1950), 75.
5. Dee Brestin, "Sally Brestin: Aslan," Vimeo video, 3:17, https://deebrestin.com/aslan.

6. Justin Taylor, "J. Alec Motyer (1924–2016)," The Gospel Coalition, August 26, 2016, www.thegospelcoalition.org/blogs/justin-taylor/j-alec-motyer-1924 -2016.

7. Taylor, "J. Alec Motyer."

8. Taylor, "J. Alec Motyer."

9. Taylor, "J. Alec Motyer."

## Chapter 7: The Surprising Way to Pray

1. Brennan Manning, *Abba's Child: The Cry of the Heart for Intimate Belonging* (Colorado Springs, CO: NavPress, 1994), 59–78.

2. William P. Brown, *Seeing the Psalms: A Theology of Metaphor* (Louisville, KY: Westminster John Knox, 2002), 2.

3. Philip Yancey, *The Bible Jesus Read* (Grand Rapids, MI: Zondervan, 1999), 109.

4. Yancey, *The Bible Jesus Read,* 109.

5. Derek Kidner, *Psalms 1–72,* Tyndale Old Testament Commentaries (Downers Grove, IL: InterVarsity, 2014), 176.

6. Karen Mains, *The God Hunt: The Delightful Chase and the Wonder of Being Found* (Downers Grove, IL: InterVarsity, 2003), 13.

7. Larry Crabb, *The Papa Prayer: The Prayer You've Never Prayed* (Nashville: Thomas Nelson, 2007), 33–35.

8. Jonathan Edwards, *The Works of Jonathan Edwards* (London: W. Ball, 1839), 902.

## Chapter 8: The Surprising Fruit of Suffering

1. Discipleship Unlimited, www.discipleshipunlimited.org.

2. Charles Spurgeon, *The Treasury of David* (1885; repr., Peabody, MA: Hendrickson, 1988), 1:195.

## Chapter 9: Our Secret Weapon

The epigraph is taken from D. Martyn Lloyd-Jones, *Spiritual Depression: Its Causes and Cure* (Grand Rapids, MI: Eerdmans, 1965), 20.

1. Dietrich Bonhoeffer, *Psalms: The Prayer Book of the Bible* (Minneapolis: Augsburg, 1970), 9–12.

2. Elisabeth Elliot, *Through Gates of Splendor* (Carol Stream, IL: Tyndale, 1981), 267.

## Chapter 10: A Royal Wedding Song

The epigraph is taken from Sara Hagerty, *Every Bitter Thing Is Sweet: Tasting the Goodness of God in All Things* (Nashville: Zondervan, 2016), 49.

1. Jonathan Edwards, *The Works of Jonathan Edwards,* vol. 24, ed. Stephen J. Stein (New Haven, CT: Yale University, 2006), 495.

2. WelcomeToTheSermon, "Mike Reeves—Enjoying Christ Constantly," YouTube video, 13:31, May 2, 2013, www.youtube.com/watch?v=NRH_E2u5cGY.

3. A. W. Tozer, *That Incredible Christian: How Heaven's Children Live on Earth* (Camp Hill, PA: Christian Publications, 1986), chap. 34.

4. Charles Spurgeon, *Charles Spurgeon on the Song of Solomon: 64 Sermons to Ignite a Passion for Jesus!* (Christian Classics Treasury, 2013), Kindle.

## Chapter 11: Holy, Holy, Holy

The epigraph is taken from R. C. Sproul, *The Holiness of God* (Peabody, MA: Hendrickson, 2010), 128–29.

1. Sproul, *Holiness of God,* 28.

2. "Read Rachael Denhollander's Full Victim Impact Statement About Larry Nassar," CNN, January 30, 2018, www.cnn.com/2018/01/24/us/rachael-denhollander-full-statement/index.html.

3. "Read Rachael Denhollander's Full Victim Impact Statement."

4. Miroslav Volf, *Exclusion and Embrace: A Theological Exploration of Identity, Otherness, and Reconciliation* (Nashville: Abingdon, 1996), 304.

5. John Eldredge, *All Things New: Heaven, Earth, and the Restoration of Everything You Love* (Nashville: Thomas Nelson, 2017), 145.

6. Catherine McDowell, "Why Do Christians Care About Qumran and the Dead Sea Scrolls?," The Gospel Coalition, February 9, 2017, www.thegospelcoalition.org/blogs/ryan-reeves/why-do-christians-care-about-qumran-and-dead-sea-scrolls.

7. Derek Kidner, *Psalms 73–150* (Downers Grove, IL: InterVarsity, 2014), 495.

8. Kidner, *Psalms 73–150,* 497.

## Chapter 12: Comfort Ye, Comfort Ye, My People

The epigraph is taken from J. Alec Motyer, *Isaiah by the Day: A New Devotional Translation* (Scotland: Christian Focus, 2011), 261.

1. "Messiah and George Frideric Handel," Christianity.com, March 2007, www.christianity.com/church/church-history/timeline/1701-1800/messiah-and-george-frideric-handel-11630237.html.

2. Alphabet Photography Inc., "Christmas Food Court Flash Mob, Hallelujah Chorus—Must See!," YouTube video, 4:56, November 11, 2010, www.youtube.com/watch?v=SXh7JR9oKVE.

3. G. K. Beale and D. A. Carson, eds., *Commentary on the New Testament Use of the Old Testament* (Grand Rapids, MI: Baker, 2007), 12.

4. *Matthew Henry's Commentary on the Whole Bible* (1706; repr., Peabody, MA: Hendrickson, 1991), 4:166.

5. Motyer, *Isaiah*, 188.

6. Charlotte Bronte, *Jane Eyre* (New York: Century Company, 1906), 337.

7. Bronte, *Jane Eyre*, 337–38.

8. C. S. Lewis, *Mere Christianity* (New York: HarperOne, 2015), 42.

9. Kevin DeYoung, "How Can This Be? A Good Friday Meditation," The Gospel Coalition, April 18, 2014, www.thegospelcoalition.org/blogs/kevin-deyoung/how-can-this-be-a-good-friday-meditation.

## Chapter 13: Homesick No More

The epigraph is taken from C. S. Lewis, *The Last Battle* (New York: HarperCollins, 1984), 213.

1. N. T. Wright, *Surprised by Hope: Rethinking Heaven, the Resurrection, and the Mission of the Church* (San Francisco: HarperOne, 2008), 104.

2. Wendell Berry, *Hannah Coulter* (Berkeley, CA: Counterpoint, 2005), 43.

3. "Home," by Drew Pearson and Blake Holden, © 2011, sung by Phillip Phillips on *American Idol*.

4. John Eldredge, *All Things New: Heaven, Earth, and the Restoration of Everything You Love* (Nashville: Nelson, 2017), 11.

5. Blaise Pascal, *Pensées and Other Writings,* trans. Honor Levi (Oxford: Oxford University, 1999), 52.

6. C. S. Lewis, *Mere Christianity* (New York: HarperOne, 2015), 136–7.

7. Eric Alexander, MP3 audio, 41:55, http://tapesfromscotland.org/Audio7/7186.mp3.

8. J. R. R. Tolkien, *The Return of the King* (New York: Ballantine, 1965), 246.

9. J. Alec Motyer, *The Prophecy of Isaiah: An Introduction and Commentary* (Downers Grove, IL: InterVarsity, 1993), 531.

## Lesson-by-Lesson Facilitator Notes

1. Mike Mason, *The Gospel According to Job: An Honest Look at Pain and Doubt from the Life of One Who Lost Everything* (Wheaton, IL: Crossway, 1994), 55.

*I am my beloved's and my beloved is mine…*
—from the Song of Songs

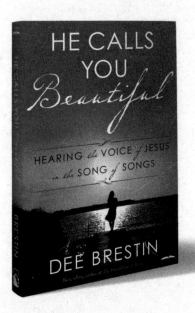

In *He Calls You Beautiful,* Bible teacher Dee Brestin explores this love song from God to reveal transformative truths for each of us, whether married, single, or widowed. With rich contemporary illustrations and insight from biblical scholars, Dee shows how God uses poetry and exquisite images to illuminate the intimacy that Jesus longs to have with you.

Includes an in-depth Bible study for use individually or in a group setting.

*"Dee Brestin has a lovely, lyrical writing voice, perfectly suited to the Song of Songs. Verse by verse, she engages each of our five senses to help us truly experience the breathtaking love of God."*
—LIZ CURTIS HIGGS, best-selling author of *31 Verses to Write on Your Heart*